OTHER BOOKS BY DAVID CARPENTER

FICTION
Jokes for the Apocalypse
Jewels
God's Bedfellows

NON-FICTION
Writing Home
Fishing in the West

How to be here? . . . How to be in the world as if it were home.

—Tim Lilburn, *Moosewood Sandhills*

COURTING
SASKATCHEWAN

COURTING
SASKATCHEWAN

David Carpenter

GREYSTONE BOOKS
Douglas & McIntyre
Vancouver/Toronto

This book is for my two Americans,
Kever and Will.

*   *   *

Greystone Books
A division of Douglas & McIntyre Ltd.
1615 Venables Street
Vancouver, British Columbia
V5L 2H1

CANADIAN CATALOGUING IN PUBLICATION DATA

Carpenter, David, 1941–
  Courting Saskatchewan

  ISBN 1-55054-530-2 (bound)—ISBN 1-55054-617-1 (pbk.)

  1. Saskatchewan—Social life and customs. 2. Natural history—Saskatchewan. I. Title.
FC3518.C37 1996   971.24'03   C96-910460-X
F1071.C37 1996

Editing by Nancy Flight
Cover design by Peter Cocking
Text design by Val Speidel
Printed and bound in Canada by Friesens
Printed on acid-free paper ∞

The quote from "Bare November Tree" from *Sticks and Strings* by John Hicks (Saskatoon, Sask.: Thistledown Press, 1988) is reprinted by permission of the author.

The poem "February" was first published in *Grain*, Vol. 23, No. 1 (Summer 1995).

The publisher gratefully acknowledges the assistance of the Canada Council and of the British Columbia Ministry of Tourism, Small Business and Culture.

Contents

PREFACE

COURTING SASKATCHEWAN IS an example of creative documentary. Nothing new, really. It means that I approach this material as a writer rather than as a historian or a news reporter. It also means that I remain truthful to the facts as I've known them, so long as they serve the story. But when real life intrudes with its humdrum little tyrannies, I tend to become creative.

Let's be honest here. I tend to lie outright. In this act of stubborn defiance I join hands with some venerable liars: Farley Mowat, who is alleged to have exaggerated some facts about his adventures in the north; Henry David Thoreau, who is alleged to have exaggerated about the extent of his isolation at Walden Pond; Paul Quarrington, who claims to be truthful about the size of his fish. This list could be extended well into next year.

It's worse than you think. This book is only as honest and fact driven as the average Canadian's tax return. I urge you to think of our personal income tax returns as a form of literary narrative. A plausible representation of real life. Rigorous about facts and figures but inventive where it needs to be.

I want to thank the people in these pages for helping me in countless ways to write this book, especially Doug Elsasser. In most cases, I have used their real names. Many good friends not mentioned in these pages, however, gave advice and help along the way. Among these were Don Kerr, Lois Simmie, John Lavery, Maria Furgiuele, Anne Szumigalski and Sandra Birdsell. The original idea for this book was hatched during a phone call from Rob Sanders. I'm indebted to Rob for making that call and for his enthusiasm along the way. I wrote *Courting Saskatchewan* with alarming speed and sent it off to Greystone's editor, Nancy Flight. It arrived in a state so finished, so complete, that Nancy only required two massive rewrites. Thank you, Nancy, for your kindly severity, your persistence and your good sense. My gratitude goes out to Ken Pivnick, teacher, scholar and wilderness man, who taught me some good things in the bush about the bush. Many thanks to the people of St. Peter's Abbey, the Saskatchewan Writers' Guild and the Saskatchewan Writers/Artists Colony Committee for my weeks on retreat to begin the first draft of this book. Last but not least, thanks to Julie Bidwell, who rises to an emergency like a trout to a fly. And that's no lie.

PROLOGUE:
THE NEWSPAPER IN THE STREET

WHEN PEOPLE ASK how long I've been in Saskatoon, I say I returned here in 1975. That's not entirely true. Until 1975 I had never *lived* in Saskatoon. But I was conceived in a basement apartment in City Park in a building still known as the Keewatin. My parents met, loved and courted in Saskatoon, and I was conceived here. I am almost the last of my mother's family to live out his life here. A bit like a salmon that returns to its original feeder stream to begin the cycle all over again, I came to Saskatoon in the summer of 1975.

That same year I had a job offer in Nanaimo, which is a beautiful town out on Vancouver Island, but I chose the job in Saskatoon. On many a winter's day, I have imagined a parallel existence on Vancouver Island that includes owning an impressive sailboat, playing a fine cello and golfing every month of the year. As things have turned out, I own a rowboat the size of a bathtub, I play the same five-string banjo I bought in 1968, and I golf so infrequently that my father-in-law has taken to sending me articles on the fundamentals of the game.

I've never been sure why I chose the job in Saskatoon over the one in Nanaimo. If economics had anything to do with it, I should have headed west to the Island and set up shop. I'm told that any property I bought around Nanaimo would have more than trebled in value. But I chose the job in Saskatoon, the small city I had always avoided in the many drives I had made across the west between Edmonton and Winnipeg.

Remember your last trip west across the prairies? Remember all those little prairie towns you raced through? Did you ever wonder what life was like in those straggling little villages? Did you race through Saskatchewan as fast as you could with visions of the Rockies beckoning like a promise of a better life? Did you succumb to the cliché that it was all so flat it was depressing?

Same here. And I treated Saskatoon as though it were merely a greater inconvenience than, say, Yorkton, because it took longer to get through.

But I chose the job in Saskatoon as resolutely as it chose me. It was a marriage made in . . . Saskatoon.

I arrived in late spring at a time when Saskatoon was experiencing a modest boom, its first in decades. Twenty years and more have passed without the slightest breath of a boom. Some economists will no doubt argue with me here, but not if they have lived in Alberta or British Columbia or Ontario, where a boom is a boom and not a mere blip on the fiscal charts.

In 1975 the vacancy rate was almost down to zero. After a lot of fussing with rentals people, I secured an apartment in the City Park district about three blocks from the place where my parents made me. I was on the second floor of a sad old three-storey frame house with a wringer washer in the basement.

I was a bachelor, and right from the start the loneliness got to me. One hot afternoon when I was walking home, I spotted a young woman in shorts on the sidewalk ahead of me. I seem to recall that she was wearing a tiny chain around one ankle. She strolled up to my old sad house and seemed to be looking for something above the front door. She stood aside as I went in and gave me a summer sort of smile. I walked upstairs and went into my apartment and heard the sound of her footsteps coming up to the second floor. I heard the sound of a key in the apartment across the hall from me and thought, well, maybe there is life in Saskatoon.

If I remember correctly, this was a Friday afternoon, and I had just moved some things into my new office. I felt that I had to get out of my little apartment in order that I might accidentally run into this woman again. So I grabbed my basket of laundry and lugged it down to the basement. No sign of her. I filled the wringer washer with a hose attached to the sink, dumped in my clothes and my soap, and pulled the handle on the ancient machine. It lurched into its old bump and grind and began the usual utterance:

leeb oip leeb oip leeb oip leeb oip

I don't remember much about the basement, except that on that hot day it was pleasantly cool and otherwise disheartening in the usual ways of unfinished basements smelling of discarded things. A dusty arachnoid feel to the place. Not an ideal spot for a conversation with the woman upstairs. I got tired of the old washer's monologue and walked up the stairs to my apartment and then walked out to the back yard and then back in again and down to the basement. Still no sign of Ms. Second Floor.

What I really needed was a *pad*. An apartment in (some might say) the bohemian section of Saskatoon near Broadway, or in a converted old mansion by the river. I needed a place where women like the one across the hall would come and go in some quantity.

playboy playboy playboy playboy

Well, that was a matter of opinion. There I was, a lonely bachelor in a grotty basement in Saskatoon being lectured to by a morally superior washing machine.

That night I lay on my couch with the fan on and the windows open. I had decided to go out and walk around the neighbourhood for something to do when I heard the sound of a clarinet. At first I thought that someone was spinning an old jazz record, which in my building was decidedly out of character. But as I listened to the stops and starts on the melody, I realized that the music was being played by someone in my building. I went out onto the second-floor landing, and sure enough, the music was flowing through the keyhole of the door across the hall. Ms. Second Floor was a jazz musician!

What would she be wearing on such a hot night? I imagined a sundress of some sort, the hem stirring restlessly in the breeze from the fan.

She was having a go at the slow and dreamy classic "Song of India." Whenever she hit a rough patch, she would stop, blow it ever so slowly, put the run together, then carry on. Instead of irritating me, these diligent attempts began to take hold of me, and finally she made her way through the entire piece with relative ease.

Something seized me, a throbbing moon feeling that her call must somehow be answered. For there was no doubt in my mind that her song was really a love call. The only analogy I can think of is that nocturnal yodelling of loons in the spring on northern lakes. If ever there was a tumescent sound in nature, that is it, and it can shiver its way through a thick fog and a log cabin to awaken you.

What else could I do? I grabbed my banjo. After a moment's tuning, I began to pick my way through a slow blues. I don't remember what song it was, but I do remember that it was drowned out by another clarinet solo, this time a slow and mellow version of "Am I Blue." She had little difficulty with this one, and I answered her with an old-timey version of "Old Joe Clark." If she didn't hear my slow bluesy number, she must have heard this lively old piece. There was a long silence.

When you *wait* to hear the loon reply, it never does; when you forget all about it, the loon cries loud enough to startle you. Very suddenly my mysterious neighbour blew out a stately version of "The Saint Louis Blues," a real performance number. My response was to do the same piece on the banjo, which involves a tricky bit of finger work with the left hand, if I do say so myself.

She answered me with "Hello, Dolly."

Back and forth we went for a half-hour or more until finally there was no response at the other end.

A bold and confident young man would have seized upon that

silence as a cue to fly over to her end of the lake, so to speak, and begin the dance in whatever way he knew how. (*That's some snake horn you're blowing there. By the way, my name's Dave.*) But I couldn't see my way clear to walk across the hall and knock on her door. What if she were with her boyfriend? What if I were too obvious in my intentions?

I went to bed.

Then it was Saturday. I was moved into my office and unpacked at home. There was nothing more to do except begin the bewildering process of getting introduced to Saskatoon—meeting and exploring and perhaps even courting Saskatoon so that this strange town that some called a city would start to feel like home.

I've lived in Toronto and Winnipeg and in various places on the West Coast. The courtship of a city often begins with an exploration of the street life. In Toronto in 1982 I felt a certain comfort as soon as I discovered the street life around Bloor and Bathurst. The same thing happened for me in Winnipeg as soon as I discovered the shops and cafés around Osborne Street. It was always the same. You discovered the street life, and you began to find out where the restless and unmarried people spent their time. And from that point on, the city, however slowly, began to make itself known to you.

And so after supper, leaving my hot little apartment in that sad old house by the hospital, I walked downtown to discover the street life of Saskatoon. If my memory serves me, it was about nine o'clock when I hit the downtown area, a few blocks from my apartment. Perhaps the busiest intersection in Saskatoon was then and still is the corner of 2nd Avenue and 23rd Street. I stood on the curb and this is what I saw. Shuffling down 23rd from the direction of the Hudson's Bay store was a small old man. He was in that near somnolent stage of drunkenness in which one seems to speak out of the confused narrative of a dream. I don't think he saw me as he lurched across the street to the corner where I stood. As he passed by he muttered these words: "Bastard thought he could throw me out with a screwdriver. A gaddam screwdriver!"

I stood there like a poet on a mountaintop awaiting a dark epiphany. Or perhaps more accurately, I stood there like those old street guys you see with nowhere to go and nothing to do. I don't know how long I waited there, but I must have been aware that I had wandered into the heart of a vast limbo, and that I *was* that guy with nowhere to go and nothing to do. I heard a faint noise coming from 2nd Avenue to my right. A ragged and dusty old newspaper was moving down the street with the wind.

For the first time I became aware of the quiet. It was Saturday night in the very centre of Saskatoon, and it was quiet because there was no one there. No traffic, no revellers, nobody. It was so quiet you could hear a newspaper drift down the street bearing the sort of news I did not want to hear.

The next day I made some discreet inquiries about the young woman across the hall. I asked another woman in the apartment below me, a perpetually exhausted party girl with a passion for the music of Kiss. She was in the habit of playing her albums very loud and falling asleep to this music next to one of her beefy snoggers from the bar. Several times already her music had left me awake until three or four in the morning, the bass notes pounding up through my floorboards with impressive authority. Her name was Doreen.

"Woman? There isn't no woman up there. Far as I know it's still just Emil. Maybe you seen his sister. She was by for a visit. She lives in Vancouver."

"Emil."

"Yeah. He's a guy," said Doreen.

"Well."

Doreen cocked her wrists in an effort to dredge up some innuendo on the subject of Emil's sexuality.

"And does Emil play the clarinet?"

"Is that what that thing's called?" said Doreen.

I guess if the guys in Kiss didn't play one, it didn't have a name. I saw Emil for the first time that day. He was heading downstairs with a load of laundry, a chubby, florid-faced young fellow. We nodded curtly at one another, as though we had been in attendance at the same riotous carnival a couple of nights before. As though Cupid had made loons of us both.

Ever since that disheartening weekend I wondered what exactly there was in this town for me. What was there to look forward to that could make it feel like home?

For a long time I've been fascinated with people's need to find a place and call it home. To do this, they embark on a courtship of sorts, a very personal voyage of discovery in which they find the *recurrent virtues* (or, if you will, the rituals) that affirm and reaffirm that place. In a newly established country (like Canada) or in a newly settled region (the Prairies), Native rituals exist, but they aren't always accessible to the descendants of Euro-Canadians and other, more recent arrivals who populate our regions. New rituals need to be invented. These new rituals need to have something to do with the land, the place that we are trying to call home. I don't mean a white man's cheap imitation of a Native ritual. Nor do I mean a falling back on European rituals as an affirmation of ethnic identity. This too can become mere imitation. What I'm looking for is a combination of the two and something else, a ritual that combines a sense of who we were with who we are becoming in the new place.

Put more simply, people need to discover things about their home that they can look forward to each year. The ultimate test, the one I've set for myself, is to recreate some memorable occasions that become so much a part of the place that each year they can be celebrated like events on a calendar of holy festivals; or, as many Native people have expressed it, rituals in response to the moons of the year: the Moon of the Hunter, the Moon of Melting Snow, the Moon of Green Grass and so on.

Every place I have lived has its rituals, daily, weekly, monthly. In Winnipeg in the early seventies, I used to walk along Main Street every Saturday morning to the many Polish, German, Kosher or

Ukrainian food shops and stock up for the week. You could smell your way from shop to shop. The little bakery on Euclid. Wawal's meats just off Main. All of ethnic Winnipeg was out to drive you mad with olfactory delights.

In Toronto in the early eighties, it made eminent good sense to stroll outside on a Sunday morning in March, buy a Sunday paper, find the nearest croissant and coffee shop, and relax with the paper for an hour or two. Watch the street life go by. If your life in Toronto was at all like mine, you wouldn't have missed this ritual for anything.

It would never occur to me to do this in Saskatoon. First of all, in March, no one *strolls* down the street, because it's simply too cold. There are no Sunday papers in Saskatoon, only a little supplement called the *Saskatoon Sun* that gets delivered too late to be of any use on a Sunday morning.

What I'm talking about here is a ritual that has something to do with certain people in certain places. Rather than dwell regretfully on what I can not do in Saskatchewan, it makes much better sense to ask what I can do. Here's where the courtship comes in, and the sense of discovery can become very exciting. What does our place provide for our delight? Our *recurrent* delight. The easiest way to count our blessings is in earthly rather than worldly terms. The air is intoxicating, addictive. The seasons are distinct—they are the four best reasons for being here. The prairie light is staggering. Everything it touches explodes into primary colours. There are countless wedges of geese, cranes, pelicans and migrating birds that fly south in the fall and return to us in the spring. There is an abundance of northern lakes so healthy and unpolluted that you can fish all day long without seeing another angler. Life around here is healthy.

I have lived here now for more than twenty years, and I've discovered some answers to this eternal search for rituals, the sort of pleasant patterns you enter when a place where you live starts to feel like home. My parents, as I say, came from here, and their parents did too. But they never taught me how to *be* in Saskatchewan, because some of them went on to other places and the others died here and were buried with their secret. I had to do this on my own, and it seems to me that I've learned something from the process that's worth passing on. Because if you can find seasonal rituals for every part of the year that you spend in Saskachewan or anywhere else, then you have found something bigger than the sum of these rituals. You've probably found a place to call home.

What do you do in January where you live? What do you do in February? If you take off for Barbados, that's cheating, and it is much too easy (if you're rich) or expensive (if you're not). Kindred Canadians, I invite you to stay home and court the season. Who knows? After one year's persistent courtship, you might just discover that there are many reasons for being exactly where you are. How else are you going to meet that special person who is rumoured to be living on the second floor?

PART ONE

Winter

Drinking Coffee in the Best Place in the World

WINTER ARRIVES AROUND the first of November. By winter, I mean permanent snow that remains until the end of March. Last year winter arrived on November 2, the Day of the Dead; this year it arrived on Hallowe'en. The proximity of these two dark and foreboding calendar days has always struck me as appropriate. The light of autumn has faded, and a sort of emotional void is revealed. The dramatic departure of light is, for some, even worse than the dead of winter, because in November all of winter lies before us, and we have to *imagine* its long and frozen reign. Bring on the SAD syndrome. Get out your copy of Malcolm Lowry's *Under the Volcano*. We're in for a siege.

The worst and most prolonged depression I ever had was in 1969. It began around November 1 and didn't leave until spring. Every November since then has borne the memory of that worst and longest winter of my life. Each November seems to argue for the same bleak condition of the soul. You cannot find a single leaf on a tree. The grass out your window and all the way out into the parkland has all gone sparse and sickly beige. The day will come when the skies turn a sort of embalmer's grey and the wind meets with so little resistance from the trees and bushes that it seems to knife through everything. If you let this grey mood invade you, you cannot for all the world imagine that the old green world will return in spring. Some call it fallow but it looks like death.

John Hicks, a Prince Albert poet, says a lot about this time of
the year in the following lines from "Bare November Tree."

The click click click I heard in the
bare November tree
was two skulls kissing

tooth to tooth a cold lovemaking.

I was reading this poem in my kitchen when I heard a rap on my
door. It was Rod Scansen. He's a young labourer with a pale com-
plexion. He wears glasses and looks more like a graduate student
in philosophy than a labourer. He was standing on my porch kissing the last sixteenth of an inch of his cigarette goodbye. I told
him I had some coffee on.

"I just heard a story on the news," he said, following me into the
kitchen. "You ever heard of Martha Justus?"

"Nope."

"You ever heard of Informetrica?"

"Nope."

"It's in Ottawa. Don't give me that bored look."

"I'm all ears," I said.

"Martha Justus is this economist with Informetrica."

"In Ottawa."

"Very good. It's some sort of think tank. You ever heard of the
human development index? I thought as much. It's a UN survey
that measures socioeconomic progress in the world. Anyway, this
woman claims that according to this survey, Canada is the number one country to live in."

"You're kidding. In the whole world?"

"In the whole world. And it gets even better. This woman, this
economist, she applies the same standard to the provinces, and
guess who comes out on top?"

"British Columbia."

"No."

"Wait a minute. What is this standard she used, this UN standard?"

"Something to do with income, education and life expectancy. But mostly life expectancy."

"Alberta."

"Get serious."

"Ontario?"

"No. You give up?"

"Quebec?"

"No."

"Labrador?"

"No."

"This is some sort of trick question, right?"

"No. Guess again."

"New Brunswick."

"No, you numbskull. Here."

"Here? Saskatchewan?"

Scansen nodded. He was hot, getting hotter. He was downright inspired.

"Scansen, nobody says things like that in Saskatchewan. Especially in November. You're shitting me."

"It gets better."

Scansen crossed his legs so that he was riding the kitchen chair sidesaddle, gesturing with his coffee mug as though it were a wine goblet. "If Saskatchewan is the best place to live, where do you think the best city is?"

"Saskatoon, of course."

"Right, and where is your favourite neighbourhood in Saskatoon?"

"Around here, I guess."

"Right again. Where is your favourite street in this neighbourhood?"

"Is this in Martha Justus's report?"

"I think we can dispense with Martha Justus at this point. Just answer the question."

"My favourite street is Temperance."

"Right again! Your street! And what is your favourite house on Temperance?"

"I think I'll go with this one, Rod."

"Carpenter, think of it. You are drinking coffee in the best place in the world."

Scansen rambled on, but I was pondering John Hicks's poem about the November tree and the two skulls kissing. In November, winter has only begun to cast its plaguelike pallor over the land: five months of cranium-freezing winds before you can take off your toque. God, I hate November.

"Say that again?"

Scansen put down his mug and held up his hands triumphantly.

"You are drinking coffee in the best place in the world."

In rebuttal to Scansen's enthusiastic insight, I read him Hicks's poem. "Well?" I said.

"Just goes to show ya," he replied.

"Show me what?"

"If John Hicks had heard about Martha Justus's report, he never would've written that poem." He broke into a self-satisfied grin. "How bout a refill?"

Why do I resist Rod Scansen's words of good cheer?

1) I am depressed.

2) All of winter lies ahead of me.

3) In every town in every province there are these people who have seen this survey proving beyond a shadow of a doubt that they live in the best, most prosperous, hospitable, progressive or salutary place in the world.

4) My depression is something of an achievement. I won't have people coming into my house and cheering me up.

5) Optimism is not/never was/never will be a viable philosophy in Saskatchewan. *Might get a crop this year.* That is optimism in Saskatchewan.

O Light, Return

ALL WEEK LONG the temperature has lingered between 27 and 42 below. One squint outside and you see a world entirely frozen. Our bedroom window is cobbed with ice crystals, the air outside is shrouded with foggy vapours from the river, and the vapours freeze in midair so that all the trees and rooftops are hoarfrosted white. The sun is gone before 5:00 P.M. At dark the hovering clouds catch the glow from the city, and the night is lurid, the frozen air pulsing with amber. When the wind blows, the trees crack and houses shriek. Every morning by 9:30, daylight is back, the walks are covered with powder snow, and the world is new and enfolded in a cold so pure and white that when you walk outside it feels like a fang descending all the way to your lungs.

You catch yourself wondering whether Saskatoon is too far north for human habitation. My mother asked the same question here back in the thirties. In winter she could see her breath in the bedroom every morning.

O light, return.

I'm up in my study, an exposed third-floor attic, a chilly room in winter. I have an electric heater by my right leg that drifts hot air up around where I sit. As long as I wear a heavy wool turtleneck over my two shirts, I will remain just warm enough to write. Later, when the sun finally rises, and if it's a clear day, the room warms up a bit. Friends keep telling me I need to insulate this attic better. They've even showed me how, but I've gotten used to the electric heater, the wool sweater, the two shirts. If my mother awakened each morning to a room so cold she could see her breath, then I can do my job up here in a chilly room.

This pigheaded resolve to live with discomfort strikes me as a particularly Saskatchewanian trait. In his fine travel book, *Saskatchewan*, Edward McCourt examines the stereotype of the western guy. "Whatever his racial origin or the social status of his forebears, [he] is a man toughened by climate, inside and out, to the texture of old cowhide. He is proud of his strength, confident of his cunning, and drunk on air all the year round."

I'd like to be that guy, but I've never quite gotten used to the cold spells, the absence of light. This absence hits me hardest in midafternoon when the sun rides low on the southwestern horizon. I peck away in the gathering gloom and try not to think of spring.

I am, of course, in dire need of a winter ritual. I need to do my Christmas shopping, I need to plan a Christmas party, I need to shovel the walk, I need to make some progress on the Great Unfinishable Novel.

Peck, peck, peck, peck. Delete.

A sudden burst of sound from the piano downstairs. Will, our son. It must be him. Picking out a tune on the old ivories. He has managed to sneak in and seat himself at the piano bench without a word. He thumps out the melody and fumbles for the harmony. It sounds as though he is fighting with the sheet music. Sometimes he does this because he wants the song to go another way, a better way.

Peck, peck, peck, peck, delete. Peck, peck, peck. Humbug. Peck, peck, peck, peck.

His tune begins to take shape. It is "Good King Wenceslas." Every time Will makes a mistake, he starts all over from the beginning. At last he's got it, his improved version. When the king bellows to his page, "Bring me flesh and bring me wine," Will pounds it out on the bass notes. When the page cries out to his king that the winter wind is too much for him and that he can go no longer, Will tinkles it on the treble notes. An old familiar carol, but now the dialogue between the great king and his faithful page has a new urgency.

Yesterday I couldn't write worth a damn. Today I can't even type. I shuffle down the stairs. As I pass Kever's door, she calls out, "Will is here to help me get the tree. You can come along if you want."

"Okay."

The whole world conspires to get me into the Christmas spirit. I stand behind Will while he finishes his piece.

"Did you know," says Will, looking up from his score, "that there really was a King Wenceslas?"

"There was?"

"Yeah."

"Who was he?"

"He was the Duke of Bohemia."

Will's lean six-and-a-half-foot frame is bowed over his songbook and his long legs curl under the piano bench. He sits in the shape of a capital S.

"Did you know," Will continues solemnly, "that Bohemia is a former province of Western Czechoslovakia?"

"Is that right?"

"Yeah."

"I wonder why the Duke was called a king."

"I don't know," says Will, again solemnly. "He was a trusting king. He got killed. He got murdered by his envious brother."

Will turns to another carol. The news about the Duke of Bohemia is anything but reassuring, but Will's music has begun to inhabit me. It reminds me of last Christmas and the Christmas before that. It reminds me of the first Christmas I ever spent with Kever, and of the very first time I ever met Will.

The piano was in the corner of the dining room of Kever's ancient apartment, a lovely old Everett of uncertain health and in need of tuning. When Kever's first marriage broke down, Will was just coming into adolescence. One of the things Kever bought with the pittance she received from the sale of their house was this piano.

She bought it for Will. He was subject to frequent fits and

depressions, and the piano was his escape and his solace. It was also a way of getting Will out of the whirlpool of his own circling thoughts. Like most kids with autism (or in Will's case, Asperger's syndrome), he was very much a prisoner of his own private world.* Kever took him to piano lessons faithfully for several years, because as a little boy he seemed to have a gift for music.

He was fifteen when I met him, but very much a child in his way of relating to the world. One day in the late fall of 1984 he was playing a familiar tune.

"What's that?" I asked him.

" 'Furry Lise.' "

I imagined a huge blonde woman with furry legs, a sort of northern amazon who sported bright red lipstick and wore a parka.

" 'Furry Lise?' "

"Yeah."

"How did she get to be so furry?"

"I don't know," said Will. "It's by lud wig von bea toven. He's from Bonn, Germany, and Vienna, Austria."

"And he liked furry women?"

"I don't know about that. Have you ever been to Austria?"

"Once."

"Did you like it?"

"Yes. It had beautiful mountains."

"Are they as beautiful as the mountains of Switzerland?"

"Yes."

This conversation went on for some time with long, silent gaps

---

* Asperger's syndrome is similar to autism and is treated by professionals as a high-functioning form of autism. People who have Asperger's are usually male. They are socially disabled because they have trouble communicating and trouble with abstract concepts. They tend to have very specialized interests and obsessions to the exclusion of the larger world and become introverted and isolated. In spite of these troubles, people with Asperger's are usually more articulate than people who have autism and are frequently endowed with special abilities.

between questions and answers. I remember it in some detail because this was probably our first real conversation. When Will was with me, he usually answered in monosyllables. He had no way of initiating conversation even if he craved it. But conversations about the places I had travelled to were much easier for Will.

"Have you ever been to the Black Forest in Germany?" he asked me.

"Yes."

"Was it nice?"

"I don't remember it as nice," I said.

Another time he asked me again if I'd ever been to the Black Forest.

"Yes. In 1968."

"Was it nice?"

"Well, I didn't see much forest."

"Was it black?"

"I don't think so."

"Why would they call it the Black Forest if it's not black?"

"Good question, Will."

Several times more, in the years to follow, Will would ask me if I had ever seen the Black Forest. I suspect that my answers were always dishearteningly vague. Each time, he seemed to be looking for some sort of confirmation from me, perhaps that the place was as enchanting as its name.

As an infant, Will would open and close the same door dozens of times. Or draw dozens of doors in his colouring book. As a little boy, travelling here and there in his parents' car, he would always look long and hard at small roads off the main highway and wonder where they went. He was born to open doors to see what was on the other side. He was born to explore enticing little roads throughout the world. Perhaps the Black Forest was like a closed door or a lovely side road, one of those beckoning names he would some day have to explore for himself.

But when I first met him in 1984, he was still full of tantrums and wild frustration. Why did his dad move away? Why were kids mean to him at school? Why didn't he have a friend? Why did nobody in the whole world understand him?

"Why do I have to go to bed?"

"Because," his mother said, "it's your bedtime."

"I don't want to go to bed."

"Will, I'll get your bath started, but when I come down, you take your bath and go to bed."

"I don't want to have a bath."

"Will? Morning comes early."

"I don't want to go to bed!"

For years Will had been given a routine that he could follow each day. Autistic children seem to cope best if they can find a routine. But now that I had come to their apartment, suddenly Will had found a guy who might be his friend. His routine was forgotten and he didn't want to take his bath and he most emphatically did not want to go to bed. He wanted to know more about the Black Forest.

He screamed and fought. He hated his bath and he hated his mother and he hated anything else in his way. Until, finally, his mother introduced the ultimate threat.

"If you don't go upstairs for your bath right now, I'll take away your world atlas."

An enraged skirmish followed over possession of the atlas, and only after that did Will go off to bed. The atlas had been the right button to push. It was his key to knowing the whole world and to being just as smart as the kids at school who called him a retard.

And now in the mid-nineties, here he was at the piano, a fine-looking young man who had left his tantrums behind. He had finished high school—somehow. He had gone on to vocational college by himself, rented an apartment in Regina, passed his apprentice course in drafting. He had gotten his first job as a draftsman in Saskatoon, sent himself to Europe (though not to the Black Forest), and eleven years from when I met him, he was playing "Joy to the World."

Kever and I applauded and Will mumbled a thank-you. He wanted to know what we would be cooking for Christmas dinner.

"I've decided to cook the Christmas tree," said Kever.

This suggestion brought a mischievous grin to Will's face. "Oh, darn, I was hoping you'd cook my favourite."

"You mean processed rat loaf? We had that for Thanksgiving."

"No."

"You must mean candied walrus whiskers."

"No."

"What could be finer than candied walrus whiskers?"

"Putty sandwiches!" cried Will.

"If you two put your coats on before I count to fifty," says Kever, "you can have putty sandwiches for lunch."

"Mmmm."

"No," says Will, unable to stop laughing. "I want lard pie with toenail crust!"

"Yuck," says Mom.

"Yuck," says Carpenter.

We hop into the car and head for Mayfair Hardware on the west side of town. Not only does this old hardware store have just about anything you ever needed for knickknacks and household items, it has a good Christmas tree lot next door. Kever has a sharp eye for a tree, and she always seems to find the best one. Will always chooses his own, a small tree for his apartment downtown. I am not there for my expertise on trees. I am there to be there.

From the moment I left the tree lot, all I could think of was let's have a party, a feast. Round up the usual suspects and stuff em into our house, but this time . . .

"Kever?"

She is admiring our tree, which now stands in the living room and awaits its first ornaments. "Yes?" she says to the tree.

"I've got an idea."

"Uh-oh."

"Seriously. For a Christmas party. Let's have an all-Saskatchewan theme. All the food should be Saskatchewan grown. All the wine, everything."

Kever seems preoccupied. She turns to me. "You mean like jellied salads and beer?"

"Yes!"

"Okay, but not just jellied salads and beer. We could serve brook trout and fried pickerel . . ."

"And wild goose with wild rice stuffing . . . "

"It could be a pot luck. And then Bob could curry some roast venison . . ."

"And Doug could do a partridge casserole . . ."

"In a pear tree . . ."

"With Father Rudolph's crabapple wine . . ."

"And we could stuff the largest trout with Doug and Barb's wild mushrooms . . ."

"And find someone with wild saskatoons to bake a saskatoon pie . . ."

"And home-baked bread . . ."

"And Will can bake those brownies he does so well . . ."

"But let's make it a solstice thing. You know, with the light coming back and all that?"

"But a feast, right?"

"Yeah."

"Yeah."

The Arcosanti Center in Mayer, Arizona, is a spiritual haven built on a mesa above the Agua Fria River valley. The people in this community have done away with the automobile and built a retreat centre that some might say is the urban vision of the future. Six thousand people will eventually live on seventeen acres in a living space of two thousand square feet.

One of their ritual meals is a vigil for world hunger known as

Frugal Soup. As Marcia and Jack Kelly, authors of *Sanctuaries*, describe it, this is a "plain meal of soup and bread, water and juice, to focus thoughts on world hunger, reminding [the residents] that even this simple fare would be a feast to some people." They see themselves as "fleas on the back of the tiger, living in a flea world on the frightening tiger of reality."

I am drawn to this form of enlightenment, I applaud it, and yet I haven't so far felt tempted to emulate it. This year, austere piety simply will not do, even if this is piety of the enlightened sort. I want an old-fashioned feast, plain and simple. This is the body prevailing over the mind. It will be satisfied with nothing less than a glorious pig-out.

And so, on the night of December 21, we will have our latest and biggest feast. I have about fifty people I want to invite, but Kever reminds me that we've never managed to stuff more than twenty people into our house. By eliminating out-of-towners, I get it down to forty. By eliminating people we've had over within the last month, I get it down to thirty. But it's no good, because Kever has measured every inch of our house and counted every available chair for dining. Twenty friends, including children— that's the limit. So I need yet another principle of exclusion. Friends who too infrequently praise my books? (No, I'd have to exclude everybody.) Friends who fish with spinning rods? (No, they're as numerous as horseflies.) Finally, I begin the job of phoning my friends, and Christmas travel takes care of a few more. I beg our friends with children to get sitters instead of bringing the wee ones along. At last we are left with twenty-three people, including Will, Kever and me.

Enter the guests. By their recipes shall ye know them.

Laureen brings local beer (Cheers Prairie Dark). Her house-mate, Catherine, brings lefse. You add just enough flour to a bowl of mashed potatoes (no lumps, please) so that the mixture will form a dough that rolls out nice and flat. Most people add a little salt to the potato mix. Roll it out, the thinner the better. You transfer this flat creation to a grill and fry it until it begins to turn a bit brown. Take it off the grill, butter it, sprinkle on some sugar or a dab of jam and roll it up. Delicious.

Judith arrives with an armful, including a baby and a quart sealer of Labrador tea *(Ledum groenlandicum)*. This tea is brewed from the leaves of a bogland shrub with hairy twigs. Its leaves are leathery and oblong, dark green on top and russet underneath, where they are fuzzy. Easily found among the northern conifers and around lakes and bogs.

Judith advises that it be picked in early summer up north when the tea is flowering. The flowers can be dried along with the leaves, and when these are brewed together they make primo tea. First, boil a big pot of water. Crush a handful of tea leaves, add them to this big pot and remove the pot from the heat until the burner cools a bit. Then simmer the brew for a few minutes longer. The tea will turn from yellow to a reddish-orange. I like to drink this tea with honey. And it's very good medicine for coughs and sore throats.

Warren and Alison arrive with a classic jellied salad and a dish known as Wild Rice Gruel. I will have to assume a certain level of sophistication on the part of my readers and skip the recipe for the jellied salad. Make it as wild or plain as your childhood memories allow. Alison's version was as fruity and colourful as a peacock in drag, but she drew the line at maraschino cherries. Warren's gruel goes as follows:

2 cups brown rice	handful shelled walnuts
1 cup wild rice	3 tbsp lemon juice
2 Norland apples, diced	1 tbsp canola oil
1 green pepper, diced	1 snowbank

Mix brown and wild rice together in 7 cups of water and cook for 45 minutes. Let cool in a snowbank. Just before serving, remove from snowbank, add remaining ingredients and toss. For a zingy variation, add one or two diced hot banana peppers.

Steven and Jill arrived with their son, Emmett (three months,

still nursing), and one of their dishes is described in the following
note by Steve:

> *I have brought grain bread, which features several products
> grown here in this land generous with grains. The bread fea-
> tures Saskatchewan whole wheat and white flour ground at the
> Robin Hood mills about a dozen blocks from my house. Other
> grain products include wheat germ, bran and flax seed, as well
> as honey gathered at T & H Apiary just outside Saskatoon. I
> used canola oil, a newly popular variety grown on the prairie
> and processed near Humboldt. The other ingredients include
> water (obviously produced in Saskatchewan), molasses, sesame
> seeds, yeast and salt.*
>
> *I was given this recipe, after tasting the bread, while dining at
> St. Michael's, a Franciscan retreat centre near Lumsden, Saskat-
> chewan, in the Qu'Appelle Valley. I was there because, since
> 1994, this has been the gathering place for about 45 writers from
> across the country, who participate in the 10-day Sage Hill
> Writing Experience held annually in August. I enjoyed the bread
> so much that I asked Joanne, the head chef, for the recipe, which
> she gave me. She in turn got the recipe from Louise Tunison.*

John and Daphne arrived with a big bowl of potato salad, and
Daphne assured me that hers was a Saskatchewan recipe, part
Mennonite, from near Langenburg, where she grew up. This
recipe passed out of print a long time ago, as you will be able to
tell from the measurements. The dressing consists of a large dol-
lop of mayonnaise, a glob of medium to hot mustard (enough to
make the final mixture "a strong yellow"), a glug of white vinegar,
enough milk to make the dressing the consistency of thick soup,
some sugar to sharpen the taste, and salt and pepper. Mix ingredients and let sit for a few hours.

Boil some potatoes, cut them up and cool them. Boil a few eggs
and cool them. Dice oodles of veggies like green onions, radishes,
celery, green peppers, red peppers and broccoli. Go for lots of

colour. (Number of oodles is up to you.) Slice up the boiled eggs and throw them in. If you've got some pickled fish in the root cellar, chop it up and toss it in.

Rod and Jeannie brought not one, not two, not three, but four Saskatoon pies. That's small *s* saskatoon, a delightful dark purple berry with a nutty-tasting centre. These are called service berries in less enlightened centres. *Service berries, can you believe it?* But here, where the plains Cree and northern Cree used them for making pemmican, they are called saskatoons, from which we get the name of our city. To this day there are jungles of saskatoon bushes right in the heart of town on the Meewasin Trail next to the South Saskatchewan River.

Here is Jeannie's recipe for a saskatoon berry pie, older even than the venerable potato salad.

CRUST	FILLING
2 cups flour	½ cup sugar
3/4 tsp salt	1/3 cup flour
1 cup shortening	½ tsp cinnamon
1 egg	4 cups saskatoon berries
2 tbsp cold water	2 tbsp margarine
1 tbsp vinegar	1 tbsp lemon juice

Combine flour and salt in a bowl. Cut shortening into flour with pastry cutter until mixture is uniform, resembling coarse oatmeal. Stir the egg, water and vinegar together in a cup with alacrity. (If the cold weather has you depressed, you can forget the alacrity.) Pour this mixture into the flour mixture using a circular motion. Stir with a fork until all of the mixture is moistened. Divide in half and form into balls. Refrigerate until ready to roll out.

Heat your oven to 425°F and roll out the dough. Line the pie plate with one of the sheets of dough. In a small bowl, mix sugar, flour and cinnamon. Stir in saskatoon berries and turn this filling into the pastry-lined plate. Sprinkle with lemon juice and dot with

butter or margarine. Cover with top crust. Crimp the edges and
cut slits in the top. Cover edges with foil but remove foil for the
last 15 minutes of baking. Bake 35 to 45 minutes, until the crust is
brown and berry juice bubbles through slits in the crust. Try not
to slobber on the pie.

Mary and Bill brought a wild rice casserole. We've done the
same dish over at our house, so I've added a couple of options.

1 handful dried morrels	1 cup chopped celery
4 cups peeled Norland	3 tbsp butter
apples	1/2 cup soaked raisins
1/2 cup wild rice	1/3 cup slivered toasted
1/2 cup uncooked white rice	almonds
1 cup chopped onion	¼ cup soya sauce

Be sure to reconstitute your dried morrels in a dish of water a
good hour before you begin to cook this casserole. Coarsely chop
apples. Add washed wild rice to 2¼ cups boiling water. Simmer
covered for 20 minutes. Add white rice, bring to a boil, reduce
heat, cover and simmer 20 minutes more. Cook onion and celery
in butter until tender; then toss in raisins and apples. Mix in
almonds and soya sauce. Bake in casserole at 350°F for 20 minutes,
or until hot.

Another delight from Judith is her wild rice bread. She has
carried this recipe all over the world, but the only place she's managed to make it work is in Saskatchewan. Note: for all dry ingredients, use dry measures.

2/3 cup wild rice	1 cup Sunny Boy Cereal
1 small handful basil	4 cups water
1 small handful oregano	4 tbsp olive oil
6 cups whole wheat flour	¼ cup molasses
4 cups unbleached	3 tsp yeast
white flour	1 tsp salt

Soak rice the night before, and on the big day, cook as per instructions. Turn on CBC Radio. Bob Kerr's show on FM seems to be best
for the action of the yeast, except on organ days. (Jurgen Gothe's
selections will sometimes precipitate premature collapses in the
dough.) Mix all other dry ingredients, except yeast. Sprinkle fast-
rising yeast over surface of dry ingredients and stir under an inch
or so. Pour hot liquid in. This is the water, molasses and olive oil.
You heat it hot enough so that you can still just barely stick your
finger in it. If you howl out in pain, it's too hot. Cover with a towel
for about one minute before mixing. (No, not your finger—the
mixture!) Work mixture about 7 minutes and form it into a ball.
Clean out the bowl, oil it, throw doughball in and let it rise until
double. Punch down and make a nest for the wild rice (well
drained). Work on well-floured surface, folding dough in on itself
constantly. Divide doughball into 3 and let rise as 3 loaves. Bake
for 50 minutes at 375°F.

Bob and Holly came early so that their Venison Madras could
be properly heated. (Madras is apparently just north of Togo,
which is east of Kamsack.) Doug supplied the venison.

VENISON MADRAS (for a real hot buck!)

2 lbs stewing venison	1 pint stock
1 oz butter or margarine	1 rounded tbsp mango
2 medium-sized onions,	chutney
chopped	1 rounded tbsp brown
2 cloves garlic, chopped	sugar
3 to 4 level tsp curry	1 cup golden raisins
powder	juice of ½ lemon
1 tsp flour	salt and pepper to taste

Trim venison and cut into cubes. Place in casserole dish. Heat butter in saucepan and add chopped onion. Sauté gently for a few
minutes to soften; then stir in the garlic and curry powder. Sauté
very gently for a further 5 minutes to draw out oils and flavour from

the curry powder. Stir in the flour. Stir in the stock and bring to a boil. Turn down to simmer. Add the chutney and then the sugar, raisins, lemon juice, and salt and pepper. Draw sauce off the heat and pour over meat in the casserole. Cover and place casserole in an oven at 325°F and cook for 2 hours, or until venison is tender.

Doug and Barb arrived from their cabin near the Duck Mountains with several delicacies, including two mallard drakes. I began to realize the enormity of this gift when I inspected the cleaned and plucked carcasses of these birds. Not only were they as fat as northern drakes can get, but there were no shot marks to be found. Either these birds had been beguiled and bewitched into a blessed swound by Barb's flute playing or shot in the head by Doug. (I never found out which.) They were stuffed with wild mushrooms, bread crumbs, onions, celery, sage and their own giblets, trussed up and roasted in an open pan for 2 hours at 350°F.

I stuffed a couple of big brookies (for recipe, see "The Place Where the *X* Is"), and Kever cooked the largest potato I have ever seen. It came from a mound in our back alley. She whipped it up in a medium-sized bowl as our mothers used to. It filled the entire bowl.

Will's brownies were a hit. Here is the recipe:

¾ cup unbleached white flour	⅔ cup sugar
	¼ cup canola oil
¼ tsp baking soda	1 egg
¼ tsp salt	1 egg white
2 cups baker's chocolate, broken into small pieces	ABSOLUTELY NO WALNUTS!
1 tsp vanilla	

Preheat oven to 325°F. Dab pan lightly with canola oil. Combine flour, baking soda and salt in a small bowl. In a separate bowl, combine baker's chocolate and vanilla. Combine sugar and canola oil with 2 tbsp water in a small pot and bring to a boil. Pour this hot mixture over baker's chocolate and vanilla and stir. Add egg and egg white and stir; then fold in the flour, salt and baking soda mixture. Pour batter into oiled pan and spread. Bake for 20 minutes or more so that brownies are just a bit underdone. (If you cook them too long, they become brittle.) Remove from oven and cut squares while pan is still warm. Let cool and serve.

These brownies disappeared so fast that Will didn't get to eat any. When the main course was over, he returned to the piano and went through his repertoire of carols. He was soon surrounded by carollers, and I was, as usual, gratified at how accepting of Will our friends are. We applauded his music and scoffed his brownies—no doubt to express our appreciation.

I was determined to give a speech at the moment all were served. When I dreamt up this speech, it seemed like a nice hostly thing to do. I would in effect say a few things about our good fortune in being here. I would thank everyone for the dishes they had brought and thank Will for the carols he had played. If I thought I could bring it off, I would thank what Doug called the Creator for all the bounty in our midst, but if that sounded too pious and grand, or more like a Thanksgiving grace, I might skip the holy bit and go on to bless the very cosmos as it did its annual magic on the solstice and brought back the light. The thing is, I was feeling so charged with the importance of my speech, I knew that as soon as I opened my mouth to express these high sentiments I would turn a nice moment into a disaster.

I looked out at Kever and Will and all our friends who are in themselves reasons for living here and said the following: "I'd like to thank all of you for coming out on such a cold night with such great food. So while the mood is on me, I want to toast all of you and invite you to drink along with me. Let us break jellied salads together for many years to come."

Before I could end with, "Here's to longer days and shorter nights ahead," Margaret began to applaud. Her husband, Guy, joined in. Everyone joined in. Knowing full well that it was the brevity rather than the speech they were applauding, I sat down at my place and tucked into the meal of a lifetime. As it turned out, even the belches were memorable.

I CAN'T FORGET something I saw on TV during the 1994 Winter Olympics in Lillehammer. A small group of Norwegians was camping in the snow in a park adjacent to the Olympic Village, and one family was cooking supper over a tiny portable stove in their tent. I think they were making soup from melted water and some freeze-dried provisions. They went about preparing their supper with a casual competence, talking about the forthcoming events as though this sort of thing were normal.

My God, I thought, those people over there—*they enjoy their winters.*

It takes some moral fibre to enjoy winter like these Norwegians seem to do so easily. I suppose there are plenty of us who would find it gratifying to watch the Winter Olympics on television while the local winter rages and pounds outside. I've certainly tried this passive approach to winter, but if I am to contend with January in Saskatoon, I need to get outside and confront the dreaded weather.

The problem with January is the cold. The fact that the sun keeps banker's hours. At the darkest time in January, the sun comes up around 9:15 A.M. and sets around 3:50 P.M. The problem with January is the ice and snow.

The problem with January is the way you breathe outside when your car won't start. You know that you are supposed to breathe through your nose; your parents taught you that. But as the air rushes down your nostrils to your windpipe, you discover that your nostrils are freezing to your nose hairs. Your nostrils begin to hurt, so you wait for the numbness to set in and the pain to pass.

Then you begin to breathe, just a little bit at first, through your mouth. What exactly did my parents tell me? *If you breathe through your mouth on a morning as cold as this one, you will freeze your lungs.*

You or your partner had meant to hang out the extension cord back in early December. Everyone else has, but until last night the weather was not quite so daunting. At any rate, not quite cold enough for extension cords. If it weren't so dark out, you'd be able to see all along Temperance Street a colourful tracery of extension cords plugged into the houses at one end and into the cars at the other end. The flow of electrons through these bright yellow and red umbilical cords is what warms up all those block heaters. The cords are suspended like Christmas decorations from the big elms, high above the sidewalks, so that you can walk under them without getting garrotted or tripped.

Inside the trunks of most of the cars and vans on our street you will find another sort of January decoration—jumper cables. Mine have red handles for negative, black handles for positive, copper clamps and nice long black cables. When one of us has forgotten to plug in for the night, we pull out the jumper cables and call on one of our neighbours to start us up for the morning. This early-morning phone call is full of embarrassed and self-deprecating asides such as *I don't know what I was thinking of* or absolute lies like *the damn thing must have shorted last night* or lugubrious confessions that border on despair like *I tell you, Carl, this winter is gonna do me in.*

Carl is my neighbour on Temperance Street. He is probably in a hurry to get to work, but I don't know this for sure; I don't want to know. He is a patient soul who on such a morning as this might well wonder at the justice of being born with such moral qualities. He must know that I have chosen him because of these qualities to be my Samaritan on a dark morning when the temperature hovers around 37 degrees below zero.

Don't ask whether this is Fahrenheit or Celsius. If you've ever lived on the prairies or in Alaska, you probably know that when it's this cold, the two systems are almost identical. Readers who are still on the old Fahrenheit system will be interested to know that when the temperature reaches 40 degrees below zero Celsius, it is also precisely 40 degrees below Fahrenheit. This is so because at this extreme low point, the two systems cross. This intersection of the two systems at such a frigid moment strikes me as a curious blend of the mathematical and the empathetic. When it's 40 below in Lignite, North Dakota, it's also 40 below in Bienfait, Saskatchewan (pronounced *bean fate, S'skatch'w'n*). When could you ever find greater empathy between nations than when their citizens' fates intersect with their systems for measuring these fates?

My neighbour Carl is already dressed and shaved, bundled up for the morning in his parka, which seems to me rather impressive for such an early hour. One look at my watch tells me it's almost 8:30.

"My God, Carl, it's almost 8:30 and it's still dark out!"

Carl looks at me the way professionals with regular hours habitually look at writers. He walks over to his car, his squeaking boots the only sound on the street. He unlocks his car, eases in, turns the key in the ignition, and it starts with only a few seconds' hesitation. His car engine is every bit as sententious as the old wringer washer in the basement of my first apartment in City Park. The engine says to me, *David, this is how a man's car should start on such a cold morning. David, this is what happens when you remember to plug in.*

I must, of course, take this bit of insolence on the chin.

When Saskatchewan people drive to Vancouver or Toronto, or best of all, to the States, they find ways of clinging to their self-esteem. In the toniest of resorts down south, Saskatchewan people will always have this secret knowledge glowing like gemstones in their souls: *We can jump-start at 40 below. We know how to drive on icy roads. We know that in January, if you've got half a brain, you plug your car in the night before.*

Carl drives past my car, makes a U-turn and brings his car to a stop about two feet from mine so that our grills are grinning at one another. Carl and I are like cattle breeders who know just what to do to promote this brief intercourse between cars. Up go the hoods. Out come the jumper cables.

Because Carl's morning has been violated owing to my incompetence, I let him do the clamping part. When our four clamps are secured to our battery terminals, I climb inside my car and turn the key. There is a guttural protest from my car, perhaps like the sound of a large grizzly with laryngitis.

As I sit in my frozen car, scraping the frost from the inside of my windows, I see that Carl is talking to another of our neighbours. With the hand that holds the now unfastened cables, he smiles and gestures in my direction. It seems that the woman down the street from us *also* needs a boost. This is inconvenient for Carl but, he explains to the woman, perhaps Carp over there would be willing to give her a boost.

It's a gentle sort of revenge. What the hell. At least now I get to be the adult, and perhaps my car will lecture her on the need to remember to plug in the night before.

Her name is Lisa, and she is off to teach a class at the university. "You absolute angel," she says to me through her muffler, as Carl's car glides up the street into the dark morning.

Like I say, the cold has descended so rapidly from the north that quite a few of us are caught with our pants down. Soon, however, there are three cars revving their engines like Lazaruses come back from the grave. Perhaps they too will pass on the gift of life.

On walking in January:

1) Kever and I cross the Broadway Bridge on our way to the downtown library. We both have on blue coats and we both have our hoods up. Frozen on the collars of both our coats is a fine pure white layer of breath. Conversation is difficult, though not impossible. She turns to me, nudges my arm, and I turn to her. Face to face, she tells me that she has no feeling in her legs.

2) When you walk out in the cold, for whatever reason, you wear boots, not shoes, and as you go, your boots squeak as though with each step you have tromped on a gopher. February's sound is more of a crunch, as though you were stepping on the *corpse* of a gopher.

3) I'm getting morbid. I've gotta stop this.

There is less snow in Saskatchewan than up in the mountains or out in the Maritimes or on the Ontario snowbelt, fewer real blizzards. There is a drier and less penetrating brand of cold, but the winters are longer, colder and more forbidding. In fact, as I've mentioned, they last for five months. Not to labour the point, but this is a long bloody time to be holed up with an afghan on the sofa with a TV set. The idea is to get out into the coldest and most forbidding stretch of winter. The idea, especially in January, is to make winter user-friendly. You can do it if you can turn the snow into your friend. That's the whole secret right there: make friends with the snow.

One way to do this is to build a great big snow hut. As a kid I had plenty experience with snow huts that were neither caves nor igloos. We would find a big pile of shovelled snow and tunnel in. My memory of such huts is that they were kind of cozy but scarcely the sort of thing you'd want to spend the night in. The Dene name for this structure is quinzhee.

Two years ago in Saskatoon, the snow was pretty abundant in January. Kever and Will and I were getting shackwhacky, so one cold afternoon I went out into the back yard and waded into the snow for my annual inspection. Sometimes the snowfall is really stingy, because winter droughts in Saskatchewan are just as common as summer droughts. But this time the snow was perfect. It came all the way up to my knees, and in the drifts and cornices around the fence and the garage, the snow was almost a yard deep. I got a scoop shovel out of the garage and began to build a modest pile right in the middle of our vegetable garden. When the pile was large enough to be seen from our kitchen window, I went inside and told Kever.

She knew what was coming. I had acquired that fanatic, other-worldly gleam in my eyes. (One thinks of that guy played by Richard Dreyfuss in *Close Encounters of the Third Kind*.) From this point on, my mood would soar or crash solely in relation to the size of that little mountain outside. So Kever set out to add her energies to the effort. Will saw this one coming and excused himself before he too was drawn in by the scoop-shovel madness.

As the days in early January went by, we were helped out by friends and neighbours dropping in. Our friend Rod Scansen dropped by to wish us a happy new year, and before the poor fellow had gotten his coat off, we had him out in the back yard with the scoop shovel in his hands. He is young and strong, so he was good for a half-hour's shovelling. Lisa, our English prof neighbour, dropped over to return our jumper cables. We tried out the ususal routine on her, which involves a pitch similar to the one Tom Sawyer used to get his fence whitewashed. She saw it coming, as they say, from a mile away. Her contribution to our project was a generous donation of snow from her back yard. Exclusive rights.

Which we needed. Our quinzhee project was moving ahead with real force now. By the end of the first week in January, the snow stack had reached a height of five feet. No one, not even the old and infirm, was safe from our entreaties. Sometimes we had several volunteers at the same time and we had to borrow scoop shovels from around the neighbourhood. When the pile grew several feet in diameter and six feet high, passersby could see it from the laneway. If we spotted them, and if they looked like they were good for a dozen or more shovelfuls, we invited them in and they too joined in on the neighbourhood project. It surprises me still to remember how *willing* these people were to be exploited. Perhaps everyone who winters in this town wants to find something to do in January.

One night in the second week of January, a strong wind blasted through our town from the west and brought with it a great accumulation of moisture-laden clouds. As soon as they hit the prairie they turned to snow and moved in on Saskatoon like a herd of albino buffalo. Day after day the snow would fall and the skies would clear, leaving behind a generous deposit of drifting flakes. This amount of snow is rare in Saskatoon. It was made to order for our quinzhee. We had exhausted our own supply of back-yard snow and Lisa's supply as well. Not only did the new storms augment this supply, they added to the snow on our private mountain, which grew to an impressive height of seven feet. One walk around the huge white pile, and I knew.

Phase two is always more creative and less exhausting than phase one. Once you have your pile, and once it's massive enough to accommodate an entire room in the upper half of the pile—a room large enough to hold several people squatting comfortably around a candle—the excavation can begin. Kever knows this from the triumphant look on my face. Without a single word, she has asked the question. I sit slumped on a kitchen chair, pausing for dramatic effect. I look up at Kever, who knows already what I will say.

"It's a go."

Kever is on the phone, and before too long all the people we will ever need are throwing on their parkas or their K-ways and preparing to come over to our place after lunch. In spite of a brutal wind outside, Kever is irrepressibly keen to be the first inside scooper.

She begins by digging down at grass level with a spade. She creates a hole just wide and high enough for her own prone body; then she probes deeper and deeper with the spade, knocking off light hunks of packed snow from inside our pile. In goes the scoop shovel and out it comes laden with chunks of snow.

Before too long, wearing her hood, Kever disappears into the hole she has made. You can see the soles of her boots less than a foot apart and, through this gap, a steady flow of snow. It's my job to stay right there, assisting the flow of snow away from the entrance and offering moral support to my mate. The neighbours who are hardy enough to stand around in the wind help to fling the quarried snow up onto the pile and wait for news from the inside. Finally Kever emerges, nostrils dripping, eyebrows frosted. It's my turn to take over.

I am thankful that Kever has had the first go at this mound. She's almost immune to claustrophobia.

Put up your hood. Come inside with me. You elbow and squirm your way in for four or five feet and look up through the semi-dark at a solid wall of packed snow. With your gloved hands or a small shovel, you scoop away, in and up. Right away you realize that your own little breathing space is filling up with falling chunks of snow, so out it must go, doggy fashion, through your legs. Your partners on the outside will ease their scoop shovels between your boots and carry off the snow to fling it onto the mound.

Kneeling now, you look up into a frozen recess. You have only been the inside scooper for about one minute. You can't turn back, even if you're good at backwards crawling. Your pride is at stake here. You must renew your assault on the snow and send it through your legs like eggs from a sea turtle and at least pretend to like it. The snow rains down on your head. You breathe it in. You spit it out. You send it flying between your legs, and if your crew is on the ball, their shovels are right there, a comforting promise of rescue if you should give the cave-in signal.

Uh-oh. What *is* the cave-in signal? You forgot to arrange it with your outside crew. Well, no matter. There never has been a cave-in. If it all comes tumbling down on your head, well, maybe you could kick and thrash with your legs and they would see your snow boots going at a frantic pace, and they would *know*, right?

Best not think about it.

I know what you are thinking. Why not just go back into the house, put on the kettle and grab a book or watch a football game on the tube?

Why not? Because if you lapse into this form of denial, you know that January has rendered you inactive. You may just as well be in Florida with the rich people. Or southern Texas or Mexico or Disneyland. And that would be cheating.

What is wrong, you may ask, with snuggling up with a good book on a cold winter's day? When you could be out there breathing in snow and confronting your lifelong problem with claustrophobia in a frozen cave?

You have to ask?

But remember, you're in there with me, scraping out an improbable dream alone in the dark, yes, alone, because there's no room for the two of us. After a while you realize that you are entirely inside the mound. If you think about it, your boots have disappeared completely from the entrance tunnel. You are now just able to kneel and look up into a burgeoning cave. Your eyes have adjusted to the gloom, and although the wind may be dismantling trees on the outside, you cannot feel even a breath of wind. You catch just the edge of that secret, hitherto unknown Norwegian feeling.

You are beginning to like this!

Once the snow that you have quarried has been cleared from behind you by your shovellers, you wriggle backwards out into the light. It's someone else's turn. And outside your little cave, it is once again cold as hell. You begin to hope that it will soon be your turn again. See? See how intrepid you have become? Someone has offered you a mug of tea from a large thermos.

It's me. I'm congratulating you for your labours. As more and more neighbours go inside and quarry more and more snow, this snow is in turn thrown onto the quinzhee, and the stack grows appreciably in width. After an hour or so of work inside, a room begins to take shape upon a floor of snow, a perfect silent white room with a rounded ceiling and a platform of hard-packed snow as flat as you can level it with your arms. Now two people can work inside, one shaping the ceiling and moving farther up and into the mound, the other sending the snow out the entrance.

At this point, you need to watch out for thin spots in the ceiling, places where the light from the sun begins to show through silvery-blue above your head. When such a place is found, you send out a piece of straw or a stem from a stiff blade of grass as a signal so that the outside shovellers can pile on the snow at precisely that spot. They will use the lightest powder snow for this, because they don't want to put a hole in the roof of your quinzhee.

Now comes the neatest part of all, the part the kids will remember for the rest of their lives. Little Gavin squirms his way in first and lights the candle. Kever follows him and brings in a big thermos of tea. Then comes Aqeel, a former neighbour who is slightly larger than Gavin. Then his older sister, Oonga, and Susan in her bright red K-ways and husband Carl. I am the last to enter, and I have the camera. I can only just crawl inside and crouch by the entranceway.

Before me is a familiar scene, one I have become accustomed to in mid-January. A happy family group—in the quinzhee it always seems to go this way. We can't help but be aware of each other's bodies as we snuggle into the rounded little room and gather around the candle. Outside it is about 34 degrees below Celsius. Inside—and you must believe me—it is about 1 degree *above freezing*. Where Kever and her American kin come from, that's 34 degrees above, Fahrenheit!

Outside, a straggle of family and neighbours are waiting for their turn. Inside, as I line up the camera, quickly, before the lens fogs over, I am almost overwhelmed by the process that has taken all these people out of the solitude and security of their homes and back in time, back through the ages, into a house of snow.

In the succeeding days, all the neighbours, all our friends and especially all the children want their turn in the quinzhee. And they want Kever and me to accompany them. We give our quinzhee tour proudly for the first few times, and then one of us gives the tour while the other makes tea for afterwards, and then, after a week or so, we just hand out the candle and let them go to it. No roughhousing in the quinzhee. No smoking. Have a nice day.

One day Will shows up. He has decided that it would be neat to crawl inside with a candle and a book. He wants the experience of reading in the quinzhee. What an ad for Literacy Week. I have already mentioned that Will is six and a half feet tall, and he has size thirteen feet. Fortunately, he is also very lean. He wriggles through the narrow tunnel and into the quinzhee with his book and candle. We hear nothing from him for almost an hour, so I go out to check up on him. I don't have to go far. As I approach the entrance to the tunnel I see the soles of two enormous boots tapping against each other in an idle rhythm.

"You okay, Will?"

"Yeah."

"Not cold?"

"No."

"Having a good read, are you?"

"Yeah."

"Do you like our quinzhee?"

"Yeah. It's neat."

The next night, Rod Scansen shows up at our door. He's been thinking about this for some time, he says. He wants to sleep in our quinzhee. I almost envy him. I've thought about it myself, but the weather has turned really cold, and the mere thought of sleeping outside in 41 below weather gives me a headache. But Scansen is all adventure. So adventurous, in fact, he hasn't brought a sleeping bag or a ground sheet or a mattress. He gives Kever a boyish and entirely winning grin. The grin means something like *My God, you mean I'll need to have all that stuff in there? Stupid ol me!*

Kever's translation of his grin means something like *Kever, mother me!*

Kever descends into our basement and comes up loaded with camping equipment. She and Scansen go out into the frigid night together with Scansen's borrowed gear. From the back window I see Rod disappear bravely into the coldest hole in all of Saskatchewan. We watch inside by the door, Kever and I. In a moment, there is a faint orange glow. Scansen's candle is lit. It will stay lit all night long, and it will be his only external source of heat. I've told him that it works this way, but suddenly I'm not so sure.

"Well," says Kever, "I guess we'll find out tomorrow morning."

Rod Scansen showed up the next morning on our doorstep. We welcomed him in with guilty relief and stuffed him full of tea and breakfast. What was it like? Oh, not bad. Not bad? Were you cold? Oh, a little chilly when the candle went out. A little chilly? How chilly? Oh, you know, a bit. And you're okay? Yeah. How did the candle blow out? I blew it out. Oh. Questions like these for a solid hour.

Kever and I must have had the same idea at about the same time, but she was braver. The next night, she was in the quinzhee. This time it was milder, about 31 below. I paid her a brief visit just before I went to bed by myself. She lay in her bag with only her nose and forehead exposed. The light from her candle illuminated the entire rounded space, and it looked much less threatening than I had imagined. Her face looked rosier than it must have been, and I knew that she would be fine in the morning. I envied her.

My own turn came a few days later. By now three people had braved the January night in our quinzhee: Rod Scansen, Kever and Susan, an artist friend. Compared with me, these are three pretty lean people. And yet in spite of being so poorly protected against the cold, they had done it without much fanfare. So I could not claim the usual accolades that come with first ascents and trips to the moon. I had to do it, and do it without ceremony. When I trudged out into the back yard with my sleeping gear, the temperature was a mere 29 below, and I had brought with me two refinements that would make my stay in the quinzhee an even more dramatic success than the nights spent by those intrepid souls who went before me: a urine bottle and a small thermos of tea.

Kever came out with me and plied me with last-minute bits of advice about how to avoid ceiling drips and where to lay my sleeping bag and what to do if a skunk strayed inside and how to keep my thermos warm all night long and how to tell what time it was when I woke up. (Pat them with a mittened hand—dripping icicles, not skunks; put it on a slant with the head slightly higher; nothing can be done; keep it in bed with you; wear a watch.)

"What if the candle burns up all the oxygen?"

"Good night, David."

"Seriously."

"Blow it out."

"How? I'll be dead in my sleep."

"Good night."

Try it yourself. You'll be all alone. You crawl forward on your belly and gape at what looks like an altar made entirely of packed snow beneath a vaulted ceiling that glows orange in the candle-light. As soon as you climb onto the snow platform where your sleeping bag lies, you are surprised at how warm the interior is. You climb up out of the cold air, which waits at the entrance. The more you stay in the quinzhee, the more your candle burns, the warmer it gets. The warm air rises to the ceiling, builds up, moves slowly downward and pushes the cold air out into the lower entranceway.

You take off your parka and boots. You take off your snow pants. If you are feeling bold, you take off the rest of your clothes, all or most of them. (On this night out, I peeled down to my long johns and socks.) You nestle into your bag and watch your breath unfold into the vaulted ceiling. You admire the architecture of it, the simplicity. You have built this thing, and at last, as your body accommodates itself to the bag and the hollows of the snow plat-form, you close your eyes.

$\mathcal{H}$ANGING OUT $\mathcal{H}$OPE
LIKE A CANTILEVER

ONE FEBRUARY, KEVER flew down to San Antonio to visit her ailing mother and distraught father. From where we were standing, it looked like an accelerated case of Parkinson's. I had to stay home and teach at the university.

One of my best students in a senior writing seminar, Brian Cotts, had written a novella about a young woman who wanders all night long through the streets of Saskatoon. I loved his setting, Saskatoon in February. Here I was in Saskatoon, reading it in February. Brian certainly captured the insomniac mood known throughout most of Canada as the February blahs. The young woman in the story wanders through a surreal landscape, in and out of her apartment, stepping over dead bodies, through trash and atrocities, and spends some quality time amid the rubble of the abandoned power plant.

We are not, as a rule, up to our knees in corpses and atrocities here, but we do have an abandoned power plant in the heart of Saskatoon. It looms over the west bank of the river like a bombed-out tenement in East Berlin. It seems to be waiting for God's jumper cables. Is there anything more poetically appropriate for Saskatoon in February than an abandoned power plant? *My* power plant had certainly abandoned me.

Brian's novella didn't get published. It had somehow shortcircuited on its own sci-fi ingenuity. But the circular journey of its main character remains, for whatever reasons, unforgettably, wondrously desolate. Perhaps Brian will salvage some of it, rework the story in some other way and publish his bizarre journey into the heart of the blahs.

It's only fair to warn you: there's a poem coming up. And yes, I want you to read it. I know. God knows how obtuse contemporary poetry can be, and life is too short to waste time reading poems no one understands when you could be out in the garage repairing your skidoo or on the sofa watching this week's edition of *American Gladiators*. I know, trust me, I've been there. I've known the anguish when you read the poem and you don't get it and all your friends *do* get it and you feel so stupid admitting that you didn't get it and you know you were the only one in the entire bar who didn't get it and later on you find out that all the others were just *pretending* they got it and who the hell needs friends like that, I mean where's the justice, eh? But in spite of the agonies we have all felt on the subject of reading poetry, I *still* want you to read my poem. I'll try to make it up to you.

I had a dream around this time, while Kever was in San Antonio. In my dream she had gone to Graceland to see the Elvis shrine. I told her how depressed I was, and she told me that I should *hang out hope like a cantilever*. Rather than try to figure out what she meant by that, I wrote the following.

FEBRUARY

In my dream I ask you when winter will end and you say when hope begins and I say when and you say whenever and I say how do you hope and you say hang out hope and I say how and you say hang out hope like a cantilever and I wake up and remember that you are somewhere in Tennessee.

On a windy February night alone in the house with your beloved gone to Graceland you don't want to catch yourself waiting for spring. It might well be spring in Graceland but you're closer to Iceland than Graceland. Don't talk to me of spring. Just let the winter be over. That will do just fine.

The snow has an icy carapace as hard as frozen bark the streets are rutted with ruts as hard as rails the ice is forever like death and taxes and hope has left the building and I've figured out why the ice is forever it's because in February it's *always* February. The wind the wind the

snowless glazing wind can't wait to get down to North Dakota for some cross-border shopping it smells like perpetual motion it smells like the track suit of a marathon runner with insomnia it smells of all the little nullities we have gathered since November it smells of waiting and waiting on a windy night until

you come home to me with a March or April bloom on your face or some evidence of returning life and you say did anyone call and all I can say is February. February. I can only pronounce this word correctly in the summertime when my lips aren't so numb and when I say February it gives my lips an aerobic workout like chewing on raw rhubarb.

All night long the sky over Saskatoon is an orange halo surrounded by all the darkness in the universe an orange as elusive as Elvis and I dream of gardens in Victoria and those tweedy voices on the TV garden shows the ones who spot an early budding rose and say oh what have we here and I wake up three four times because you are not here and in my dream I am

always waiting for winter to end. Melt is a word in someone else's lexicon all over the yard and down the lane and out across the prairie snow is a glazed expanse for the wind to sail past the snow wants to be ice but it can't the ice wants to be snow to lie as elegant as snow should lie it only wants to be what it can never be and so do I.

So I lean out hope like a cantilever
less for the cant and
more for the lever
the heart says soon
the wind says never.

If you have never lived in Saskatchewan or on the northern prairie, I need to reiterate that February is not the second month of winter, not the third month, but usually the *fourth* month of winter. It almost never reaches 40 below in February, it doesn't very often reach 30 below, but in February winter turns from a snowy hold to an icy grip, from a hoarfrosted white to a metallic grey landscape. The February blahs are a response to the sheer length of winter up here, to this clenched landscape and to the absence of light. The light has been returning, technically, for about five weeks, but who wants to go outside to notice it?

Not me. I get up in the dark, go to work in the dark, come home in the dark, rattle around in the house from basement to third-floor attic, play solitaire compulsively and watch television reruns during bouts of insomnia. In the second week of Kever's trip to San Antonio—where she was dealing with something closer to the abyss than the blahs—I took out a video by Woody Allen entitled *Shadows and Fog*. Perhaps I chose this video because the title in some way correlated with my mood. In the movie a killer is loose in the city, and all night long the characters stumble around in the dark and the fog trying to organize a defence against the killer or looking for someone while the someone they are looking for is either in danger of getting murdered or looking for someone else. It's Woody Allen's darkest comedy, the nightmare Ingmar Bergman might dream in New York in February.

This movie, which I intend to watch again *next* February, is oddly reminiscent of Brian Cotts's unpublished novella. It made me want to walk around Saskatoon that night to discover the joys of February and plumb the depths of my own February blahs. It made me almost yearn for the abandoned power plant on the other, sadder side of the river.

I shut off the TV set and put on my parka and boots. It was just past midnight, 20 below with no wind. The night sky was obscured by clouds and river vapours, and an oppressive fog had moved up from the river and into the streets. To me, it seemed, *several* layers of darkness were presiding over our heads. The congested sky picked up the reflections of the lights from downtown Saskatoon and glowed dark violet and orange.

I walked out to Saskatchewan Crescent and looked down on the bridges and the river. I couldn't make out the river at all, but I could see some of the lights on the Broadway Bridge, which is the closest bridge to my house. The downtown lights and lighted windows and neon signs swam together in a soup, like illuminations through a smudged and frosted window.

I crunched along, wrapped in a wondrous gloom, the only insomniac outside in all of Saskatoon, and walked along the Meewasin Trail under the Broadway Bridge. I might have been wary of muggers, but it was absolutely too cold for muggers. Long winters are merciless on nocturnal criminals; perhaps they all avoid Saskatoon—except for the mentally challenged. With some assistance from the feeble street lights, I managed to find the walkway on the Victoria Bridge and to walk across the river past a shrouded and frosty statue of Gabriel Dumont. He hunches over on his horse as though wondering what has happened to the Saskatoon hostelry, and I crunch past him to the freeway overpass.

(If you are fond of contemporary Polish music, you might want to put on something by Górecki at this point.)

The freeway overpass partly obscures the abandoned power plant. This one has all the charm of freeway overpasses throughout the continent. Great place for an assignation with the postatomic mutant of your choice.

I trudged beneath it and up to one of the high fences surrounding the old power plant to muse on the squalor and gloom of it all. The night was so entirely congested with fog that I could only see the lighted buildings on either side of the power plant, but the site itself was just a gap of darkness. What I *might* have seen were its rusty girders, broken and boarded windows, walls of red brick and concrete, green and empty storage tanks and huge insulators, and on the ground, the tall bent husks of weeds that grow above your head in summer.

I was drawn forward through a tear in the fence by some sort of world-weary fascination. I began to walk around among the rubble as though I had been transported into a *film noir* and had to play out my part. A voice from outside the fence cried, "Sir?"

An unmistakably official voice.

"Sir?"

My *film noir* was apparently over.

I retraced my steps and walked into the beam of a policeman's flashlight.

"Are you looking for something?"

"No."

"Well, sir, this is private property."

"I was just . . . thought I'd have a look at the power plant. I'm not a . . ." I was looking for a nondefensive way of saying *I'm not a crook.*

The policeman came to my rescue. "Jeez, for a second there, I thought you must of been the coach again."

"The coach?"

The policeman mentioned the name of an amateur hockey coach. "Every time his team loses a game, he comes down here and paces around till all hours."

A hockey coach, my kindred spirit. Perhaps I wasn't the only insomniac out at night. The next time I get the blahs and come out here, I will be prepared to discuss the virtues of aggressive forechecking and a good team attitude. And perhaps our coach, if he's still with the kids this winter, will have to listen to some existential grumbling. I'm sure we'll part the richer for the experience.

But I had the blahs that night and they wouldn't go away. The problem is, the blahs don't compel sympathy like the blues do.

The blahs don't have a rich and sad musical tradition behind them. Any reasonably modern, neglected, atonal symphony will do. The blahs are one of the great unsung emotions.

Kever in San Antonio, caring for a sick mother and an over-wrought father—she had the right to sing the blues.

But the blahs, they are considered a lower-order emotion until they turn into something worse. When we are beset by the very worst of February emotions (boredom, depression, despair), we can either flee them (fly to Bahamas, have affair, shoot exotic animals on redneck game preserve), which can turn out to be expensive, or we can confront them and let them run their course (do anything that correlates with your despair: take night strolls to garbage dumps, graveyards and abandoned power plants; watch MTV rock videos). If you confront your mood and live through it without trying to alter it with drugs or any variety of false and desperate cheer, if you let it run its course, you might just discover, as I did that night, how truly insignificant you and your little neuroses really are.

February in Saskatoon is a very good time and place for such discoveries. After all, as Jungian psychoanalyst Robert Brosnak has said, winter is a time for introversion. A lot of people have trouble with that because we live in a very extroverted society.

I suppose it was difficult for me to leave the warmth of my house and wander out into the night in search of squalor—any vision of Saskatoon that correlated with the mood I was in. But if *that* was difficult, imagine trying to explain my motives to a wife come home from her mission of mercy.

"So, you had this sudden idea you wanted to see our power plant at two in the morning." Her head is on my lap and a mug of tea is resting on her belly.

"Yeah."

"Why?"

"Well, at first I thought it was that long thing by Brian Cotts."

"That long thing."

"Yeah. And then I thought it was maybe that Woody Allen movie."

"What movie?"

"*Shadows and Fog.*"

"I heard it was kind of depressing."

"Well yes, it was, but it was just what the doctor ordered. I mean, I sort of really got into my blahs and sort of went with it. Sort of?"

"I see," she said, the way people do when they haven't the slightest idea what you're talking about.

It was good to have her home. She was obviously glad to see me. I could hear her rummaging happily in the basement. I began to feel the beginnings of sanity. My abandoned power plant world was beginning to fade like a nightmare. I almost began to doubt my conversation with the policeman. Kever returned to the living room, holding two pairs of skates.

"Why don't we?" she said. "It's only 18 below."

When Kever was old enough to skate, she was growing up in places like Salt Lake City, Louisville and the Philippines. When she moved to Saskatoon from Arizona in 1975, she was a devout non-skater. But when she met me, she thought she should give it a try. This courageous attempt to learn how to skate coincided approximately with her decision to take out Canadian citizenship. Several of her more ice-wise male friends, including me, were enlisted. We took turns lurching around the pond with Kever between us, like dancing bears on linoleum, and she soon got the hang of it—enough, at least, to think about a solo flight.

A word or two about our pond. It is really little more than a one-acre, well-flooded depression on the grass along Spadina Crescent in a small park just north of the Bessborough Hotel. This is a CPR hotel built a long time ago on the model of a Loire Castle. It seems to preside over the pond and its skaters, giving the outing a sort of Old World atmosphere. Old World, that is, except for the sound system, which is plugged in to a local pop music station. There is a small changing shack with a stove in the middle, and the shack is usually full to overflowing with kids and their parents. To add to the frenzy of children's voices, there is the irrepressible quacking of deejays on various topics like winter-wear specials and where to get the thickest pizza in town.

This is almost the only setting I can imagine to celebrate February. Skating this pond is much less exhausting than a ski loppat or a trapper's festival. You grab your skates and just follow the Meewasin Trail along the river until you hit the Bessborough. You do this, quite possibly, for the same reasons you might build a quinzhee in January. If you can make the snow your friend in January, then surely you can also make the ice your friend in February. Ice doesn't have to be the reason you flee to sunny Florida. It can be the thing you glide on in sunny Saskatoon.

Which brings us to Kever's solo flight. There came a time in her training period when Kever could manage with just me to hang on to. Then she progressed from clutching my arm with both hands to holding my hand in the normal way. And then, on this February morning of hoarfrost and blue skies, she suddenly let go of my hand. I was flabbergasted.

"Don't go," she said.

She charted a careful course around the pond's little island, and I followed beside her. I noticed that she kept her right hand extended, as though still holding on to an invisible partner, so I did the same with my left hand. There, we had it. With hands extended towards each other, just in case, we skated slowly around the pond. A stranger might assume that between us was the ghost of a lost child. I'm not sure how many turns we did around the pond. Perhaps three.

There was one rule I had to adhere to: do not gush about how well the skater is doing. In fact, do not say a word about anything. Kever's maiden solo flight seemed such a fragile thing, her body in a constant negotiation between the vertical and the horizontal, that even the slightest bit of encouragement would shatter her concentration. I faded slowly away from her side. She was wrapped in her own dream.

It must have been a particularly Canadian dream. If the American dream is the spectacle of flying to freedom and success, the Canadian dream is one of not falling and making a spectacle of yourself. Yes, Kever's was an entirely Canadian performance. Not once did her face relax into a victory smile.

Not until she was sitting safely on one of the benches at the side of the pond. Then she allowed herself a brief histrionic gesture. Eyes closed, fists clenched, she whispered, "Yyyyyyes!"

Fourteen Vignettes and
an Ounce of Civet

1) A TIGHT LAYER of granular snow and its beadwork of ice lay all over Saskatoon, and once more our back yard seemed to glow white in the dark. The wind moaned and sighed melodramatically all night long.

The blizzard continued, the snow piled up higher and higher, and the wind blew into yet another stormy day. After a very long time, the snow turned to flurries and the wind dropped to twenty miles per hour. Many times during the third and last day of the storm I found myself staring out the window.

Early on the third morning, huddling in bed, I caught sight of Gus, our tabby, staring out the window. Right next to me Kever was staring too. What a sight to behold: the three of us, man, woman and cat, all staring out at the pure white world of wind and flurries, rendered immobile like people in a painting by Alex Colville. All waiting for the same thing. For winter to end.

2) From February to March we move from blahs to yearning. This is not the first month of spring but the last of winter. I always wander through March in a state of unarrested yearning. Already my mind is wandering and I'll just have to follow it.

3) Yesterday I read an American commentary on the Bernardo-Homolka murders. Americans have been watching bits of the story down there on TV while we wait up here under a media blackout for the trial to get under way. I suppose the blackout will

serve to keep those lurid details out of some people's minds for a while. But they've entered my mind, the horrors those girls went through. What their families are going through.

I am reminded of my boastful claim that we in Saskatoon are not exactly up to our knees in corpses. Never wash your clean laundry in public. Now there is talk on local radio about the slaying of four women from Saskatoon. Shelley Napope. Eva Taysup. Calinda Waterhen. Janet Sylvestre. Murdered. Some sick troglodyte is out there wandering our streets. *Give me an ounce of civet; good apothecary, sweeten my imagination.**

4) February in Saskatoon is so spectacularly dreary, and April so dramatically melty, that March suffers the fate of certain talented actors without star quality. What is the nature of March? Why do I respond to things differently in March from the way I do in the more welcoming months? I go to bed at night with gothic spectres of dread and wake up wondering where they came from, where they've gone.

No escaping it: they came from the newscasts and they've gone looking for more atrocities, more victims.

5) *Wanuskewin* is a Cree word meaning 'seeking peace of mind.' It is the name of a sacred place in a coulee a few miles north of Saskatoon. For thousands of years a refuge for plains aboriginals to winter in, this lovely coulee is now dedicated to the cultural legacy of these people. It is indeed a good place to seek peace of mind.

6) Yesterday I drove out to Wanuskewin through a brownish-grey sorbet of slush, past dazzling fields of fresh melting snow. Over one field a large ominous dark bird was flying. At first I thought it was a crow. I'd already seen several that week, my first of the year. But this bird was much too big for a crow or even a raven. A

---

* This quotation is from *King Lear* (Act IV, scene 6, lines 132–33).

golden eagle? No, the neck was too long. A greater Canada goose? No, too early.

At last I arrived at the information desk face to face with three young Native women. They looked like university students.

"Who can I speak with about seasonal rituals among the Plains Cree?"

"Seasonal rituals, eh?"

"Yeah. Late winter rituals, actually."

"Late winter rituals, eh?"

"Yeah. Like March?"

"March!"

"Bummer of a month."

"Yeah."

"You should talk with Vance," one of them said yearningly.

"Vance McNab," said another.

"Yeah, he'll be around here sometime this morning."

"How would I recognize him?"

"Oh, he's this Cree guy and he's really tall and he's got this dark curly hair—"

"His eyes are the bluest blue it's no it's like it's like—"

"Royal blue."

"Yeah, royal blue, he's got these amazing eyes, they just look at you and it's like—"

"Thank you."

I went to the cafeteria and had coffee. A tall young man approached my table. As he came nearer, I squinted hard to see if his eyes were royal blue. He must have thought I was half blind or barmy. The man was Vance McNab, and he is director of visitor services at Wanuskewin.

"Well," I said, trying to ease into the conversation, "here it is, March already."

"Yeah," said Vance, smiling. "Bummer of a month."

"Yeah."

Before I could ask him precisely how March was regarded among the Plains Cree—and I swear this all happened—a small wedge of Canada geese flew past the cafeteria window. Vance couldn't see the flock because his line of vision was away from the window. At that moment I realized that the large bird I had seen flying over the field had indeed been a Canada goose.

Just as the wedge of geese was passing out of sight, he said, "March is the Goose Moon."

"What?"

"March. It's the Goose Moon. The Moon of Returning Geese, as the elders like to say."

7) I must always have known. The first hopeful, haunting moment in March is when the first geese fly over your street. According to the Plains Cree, January is the Great Moon, February the Eagle Moon, and March the Goose Moon. One of Vance's March rituals is to watch the great flocks of returning geese circling the creek that drains the Wanuskewin coulee runs into the South Saskatchewan River. Every March, a big stretch of river is open well before the ice melts on the sloughs. Big flocks of greater and lesser Canadas use this open spot as a first landing strip and fly up through the coulee to feed in the fields. They use this coulee for the same reasons people did hundreds and thousands of years ago. Refuge from winter.

Again and again I'm confronted by the elusive sense of creaturehood that unites people and animals. Yearning people and yearning animals. Yearning for winter to be done.

8) Catherine Macaulay and Laureen Marchand are visual artists. They have a house in City Park, their walls adorned with paintings by their contemporaries. They are both former librarians, and they both quit their full-time jobs to become painters. A breakfast in their house is always a treat.

On this fine Sunday morning, a sort of hushed frenzy is radiating from their conversation. Even their cats seem to take an interest. Seed catalogues cover the breakfast table. They've all recently been to Gardenscape, Dutch Grower's annual garden show. In spirit they are already in their garden, urging their shrubs along in the luxuriant warmth.

"When do you usually start your tomatoes?" Catherine asks Kever. "They were so incredible last year."

"I've already started mine," says Kever. "I started them two weeks ago."

To be accurate, I should place an exclamation mark at the end of each of the above utterances. I am not fond of these things; they are too Pavlovian for my liking. (Place exclamation here, reader slobbers with excitement. Place *two* exclamation marks here, reader will fall off chair with excitement.) But this is precisely what a bright day in March will do to human speech in Saskatoon. Conversations about the most ordinary things will be littered with exclamation marks. It must be the returning light.

"Lorna Russel gave me some leftover bulbs!"

"You mean for the jumbo crocuses?!"

"Yes!"

"No!"

"The ones she got from Cruikshank's?!"

"Yes!"

"No!"

"I kept them in the pantry!"

"In the pantry! That's where I keep my iris bulbs!"

"Can you believe how cold it was yesterday!"

"Tell me about it!"

"Bummer of a month!"

9) I have my own favourite Theatre of Yearning, my equivalent to Gardenscape. It's the Annual Outdoors Sports and Leisure Show. Both shows arrive in March, about the time the first crows appear. At the Sports and Leisure Show you can get your fill of speedboats and luxury trailers and compound bows and wildlife sketches. You can talk with northern fishing guides and bear hunters, wild-crafters and trackers. You can drift through a forest of pamphlets on northern canoeing or learn how to get boneless fillets from a

northern pike. You can fill up on sugared bannock, mooseburgers, thirty kinds of fudge. You can shoot rapids on video, shoot at targets with an air pistol or just shoot bull with one of the resort hucksters.

I usually start the day by heading for the Kilpatrick Flyfishers' display. There will always be a fly-tying guru surrounded by troutaholics. There will always be a healthy flow of information and theories about good lakes to try, and about big lunkers that just might fall for an olive hare's ear or a green woolly bugger. This information and the passionate talk about lunkers are every bit as intoxicating as garden talk.

The highlight of my day will be at the Saskatchewan Environment and Resource Management booth. Not only will they have a glass tank filled with live brown trout, brookies, rainbows and exotic trout hybrids . . . (Pause for breath. Prose becoming tumescent. At any moment exclamation marks will begin to re-appear.) . . . but best of all, they will be distributing the annual "Fish Facts" bulletin. This is a summary of all the stocking, netting, and creel census stats—in other words, a summary of all the results of last year's fishing probes in the province. I read these stats with the obsessive attention one usually associates with aesthetes and poetry lovers. No, don't laugh. Just read a sample from a recent issue of "Fish Facts."

> Sands Lake   northeast of Mistatim
>   netted 36 brook trout
>   250 to 1475 grams
>   netted 4 brown trout
>   2000 to 2200 grams
>   stocked in 1992 and 1993 with
>   browns and brooks
>   limited angling activity to date

Are you not drooling? Note the reference to *limited angling activity.* This means that you could be one of the first anglers to lead one of these monsters into the net. You could be a Columbus among fly-fishers. How could a mere poem vie with this list for sheer hypnotic power?

10) I am spooked, a victim of atrocities on the evening news. I can't escape the conviction that life in the world has become cheap and perilous. I'm sulking around the kitchen at three in the morning, waiting for signs of world anarchy to penetrate my neighbourhood. It doesn't take a shrink to diagnose this one: I'm inventing an epidemic of evil out of the pathetic evidence of our newscasts. You have to combat this neurotic horse-shit kind of thinking. There's enough real gloom out there without manufacturing more of it. Must get out more.

Melt, damn it! Melt!

11) March has cast a spell on our house. Kever answers with seedlings. On every available window ledge, any receptacle of sunlight, she has placed her trays and pots. Starters, we call them. In March we start things. Tiny seedlings no bigger than blades of grass. Kever's tomatoes are fragile hopes that some day will bloom in the back yard. Say "Tomato salads" and the word becomes flesh.

12) I take home my "Fish Facts" pamphlet and read it in bed at night. Kever might say something perfectly reasonable, like, "This spring, let's rototill a week earlier."

I will look up from my "Fish Facts" and see her face, but just as my response is forming, a large brown trout will drift casually between us and tail off into the deeper water.

"What?"

"I said, let's rototill a week earlier this time. In fact, let's rototill at the end of April. Susan D'Arcy does."

Another trout swims by, then flirches right above my head to grab an emerging caddis. A brook trout this time. Quite possibly it had been hiding in the folds of our blankets. You can tell it was a brook trout from its orange flanks and olive-green back. A plump foot-long brookie just right for the pan.

"Last year the snow was gone by the first week in April, or at least most of it. Remember?"

"Oh. Yes. The snow. Yes."

"You don't remember, do you. What are you looking at?"

We don't have communication problems; we have problems with trout swimming through our house in March.

"Are they . . . back?" she says.

"Yes. I'm afraid so."

"Oi."

13) No sooner do the trout appear, than they return to their lairs beneath the ice and venture out only in dreams: perfect, uncatchable, taunting like sirens. But the geese are as real as the cankered ice and grimy snow. They seem to precipitate the end of winter. All along our street, the word spreads: the geese are coming in. You can hear them over your house at night. Their frenzied falsetto barking comes closer and closer as they set their wings for a mass landing on the river.

14) It's seven o'clock in the morning and light out. Light in the early morning. A small victory for humankind. I'm doing Saturday errands. I drive home yawning at the newfound morning light. The sky is clear, the wind a mere puff, the air willowsweet and bracing.

Oh, yes. Must pick up a *Globe* at the whutzit box down the street from our house. CBC morning show on my car radio. George Shearing plays "Mac the Knife" on the piano. Reflectively, he plays, tenderly, as though picking out just the right chords of consolation for a hangover. It sounds like that unguarded winding-down session just *after* a jazz concert. I can not get out of the car to buy my newspaper. I just sit there hypnotized and listen.

Shearing plays it so very slowly. Perhaps he is demonstrating each chord to aspiring pianists. A song I've known eons before Bobby Darin did it in the early sixties. But has Mac the Knife ever been so alive and meditative as he is right now? Could you add anything to this moment to make it more perfect? Is this what the mystics describe as that instant before the onset of prophecy? If so, where will the prophetic words come from?

The *Globe?*

I wind down my window, open the car door. Coins in hand, I take three or four steps in the direction of the whutzit box. Shearing's languid notes follow me out my car window and bop across the street, bouncing in slow motion off the windows of the Soul Kitchen. I watch the notes as they wobble back to me, a little discordant but still on course, improv dancers on holidays. Because of the frost on the glass, even when I squint at the little window on the whutzit box, I can't make out the headlines. So I slip in my coins and yank open the little window—*Bernardo Trial on Hold.*

Get the hell out of my life.

It's not in the headlines, so just when I've abandoned the search for my epiphany in the *Globe & Mail* it comes to me without words, a clamour in the sky, louder and louder, the ultimate expression of yearning.

Honk-a-honk!

Seventeen Canadas, calling low and musical into the jazzy morning, seventeen saxophones with laryngitis, holding a perfect V, one at the apex and eight on either wing, and not there for me alone. More likely dropping by to jam with George Shearing, who knows that the shark has pearly teeth, Babe, and that he swims among us, so why not just stick the little predator into a song and forget the headlines for one perfect moment?

Peace, brothers and sisters. Honk on by.

PART TWO

Spring

THE ULTIMATE DANCE

IN A *LIFE* magazine I have long since lost track of there's a black-and-white photograph of a group of Russian women, circa 1960, coming home from work around the first day of spring. They are big women, middle-aged or older, and they are standing at a bus stop with their shirts open and their large breasts bared to the sun. (Kever remembers them as wearing brassieres, but I'm not sure.) Not one of these women strikes me as ostentatious or coy; they are all, it appears, just enjoying the sun for the first time in many months, and in that moment of perfect response to the long-gone sun, a photographer was there to record their propitiations to the sun god. I've never seen a photograph that speaks more eloquently of the return of spring.

Spring up here, spring everywhere in the north.

On the subject of spring in Victoria, poet Susan Musgrave wrote the following paean in *West* magazine: "When the rest of the country is dyeing the snow green for St. Patrick's Day, we're up to our short-sleeved 'Super, Natural' T-shirts in daffodils. There's this warm-earth-budding-emerald, wild onion, and soft rain smell." Throughout my school years, I was always perplexed by such musings. There's a whole tradition of warbling about spring draped in lush and verdant hues that comes from dewier places than the prairies. The descriptions of spring from these places seemed so exotic and tweedy as to stretch the bounds of reason. Oh, to be in England now that April's there, intones Mister Browning. How could I not be impatient with his April elms in leaf and his chaffinches singing in the orchard?

Later in my life, after enjoying a whole slew of spring days on the West Coast, in England and in the United States, I came to believe that spring was something that other people experienced and from which I had always been excluded. God knows these springs were nothing like what passed for spring on the prairies.

But on the spring question, as it relates to people up here, I have changed my mind. It really does exist, I'm now convinced. You just need to be quick to see it because, as we say here in Saskatchewan, it moves faster than shit through a goose. And you need to know how to rejoice in a northern prairie spring on its own terms. One day on a Regina CBC show, I was asked to compare notes on spring with my friend and fellow writer Guy Vanderhaeghe. The date was March 21, and as usual winter was still very much in evidence up in Saskatoon. Real spring usually came in April, we both agreed.

How do you know when it's spring? asked our host.

Guy began to tell the host, who was probably not a Saskatchewan native, about spring coming to the town of Esterhazy (in southeastern Saskatchewan) and the Vanderhaeghe farm nearby. He always knew it was spring in town, he said, when the ice melted on the town rink, which meant that there would be no more hockey or curling. He always knew it was spring on the farm when a large manure pile next to the barn began to melt, attracting a new crop of flies. In town, you saw spring arrive with perplexing speed; on the farm, you smelled it coming.

Exactly.

There are usually three or four false springs in Saskatoon, running approximately from late February to late March. One kind of false arrival might be a leftover chinook blowing in from Alberta, or even a serious melt of several days. Take heed: nature is merely playing with you. Outsiders to this cruel game will put away their winter clothes and wear something brave and daring, the latest spring fashion, say, and gambol happily down Broadway in running shorts or tank tops—perhaps a little like that fawn in the "Bambi Meets Godzilla" cartoon. Beware. Winter has not finished with you. He always has one or two blizzards left in his arsenal.

Three or four melts followed by three or four head-numbing

storms. You need to expect this sadistic game, perhaps even exult in it. Cheer for Godzilla. Really, it helps. _Refuse_ to put away your winter garb. Stand before the mirror on the sunniest day in March. Recite, before the mirror, once a day, _As flies to wanton boys are we to the gods; they kill us for their sport._ Only then can you be happy in the fifth month of winter.

And then it comes. Spring and April, April and spring, like glamorous lovers to a party. Oh, were you people waiting for _us?_

The first thing I notice is that all the grimy ice on the roads and sidewalks feels exhausted under my feet. Right around then, the streets begin to flow. Everywhere you walk, miniature rivers of sandy brown water cut channels into the melting ice. The kids build dams and wait for cars to sink to the bottom. The bigger kids make snowballs and wait for anything that moves. This revelry and the big melt last for maybe a week, and suddenly the streets are dry, the boulevards unclothed and derelict. All the garbage you could forget about beneath the snow, all the boxes of Kentucky fried chicken and styrene fast-food containers and dog turds and discarded condoms are laid bare by the scavenger wind. All the sand from the city trucks, heaped on the winter ice to make the streets drivable, all the mould from dead leaves, all the dreck from five months of huddled living lies at your feet as you walk down the streets. Ah, smell the rank spring air.

The wind loves its role in springtime with surpassing glee. It gathers up all the grit and sand on the streets and blasts it into your face. You come home with spring in your teeth. Regular flossing helps.

I suspect that even people's dreams are moulded and reshaped by spring. I dream of trout rising, trout spawning, trout swimming past my feet in two feet of clear water. I can never catch them because I can never get my line into the water or I can never manage to get out of the car because someone wants me to pick up their income tax form at the post office and when I arrive back at the magic stream it has become a strip mall and I don't have any clothes on and when I find some clothes someone has stolen my fly rod. For some reason, Kever dreams of trying to catch a bus or a train or trying to reschedule a flight and of not being able to find a coin for the pay phone or of trying to arrange a meeting she doesn't really want to go to and getting there on the wrong day.

One of my rituals for April that allows me to contend with all these less than tidy things blown around by the sandblaster wind is the Welly walk. You tug your Wellies on over a pair of thick wool socks and tuck your pant legs inside. The more you walk in them, the more your socks tend to ride down your ankles and bunch up around your heels, but that too is all part of the Saskatoon Welly walk. We start at our own back alley and work the alleys two or three blocks from the river. The alleys closest to the river are too fenced up or decorous for snooping. But the alleys where we live are just about right. All the things your neighbours have thrown out over the winter or are trying to hide can be found in the alley. Expired cars, mouldy mattresses, weedy gumbo, unrecycled garbage and usable items like old lumber that bring out the scavenger in you.

If you like to watch birds, you might notice that the crows and gulls are embarked on similar scavenging missions. They are amazingly clamorous, the crows throughout the day and the gulls at night. These birds create a flyway to and from the town dump.

The things they must know about us—all about our discards and dirty secrets, our expensive and wasteful ways. It's a wonder they show us any respect at all.

So down the alleys we go, envying this man's trellises, that woman's compost box, planning what we could really do with our back yard, like those people with the brick veranda and the lily ponds. And isn't that what Catherine and Laureen mean by a shade garden? The puddles are cool and sometimes covered with thin sheets of ice, and the idea is to break as much ice as you can because it's April.

On one April Fool's Day, Kever left her first husband.

On another April Fool's Day, she moved in with me.

In April, Bob Calder and I plan our spring fishing trip.

In April, when all the ice is gone, we call up a fellow with a rototiller. About the last day of April, he will till the garden in our yard, Mrs. Jenkin's yard, Carl and Susan's yard and Lisa's yard.

In April, yearning turns to action.

In April, tumescence is more than just a fancy word.

In April, university students hurry to their last lectures and their exams with a resignation that would do credit to the great martyrs.

In April, the river begins to rise.

In April, the sharptails dance. Yes, the sharptails!

Steven Smith came from Toronto to Saskatoon in the late 1980s for a few weeks of poetry writing at one of our retreat centres for writers and artists, and he stayed. He has a bushy dark moustache, and his hair is long and curly, real vintage Three Musketeers. He's a born-and-raised urbanite with a growing appreciation for the less than urban. In recent years, he's been living with Jill Robinson, a fiction writer formerly from Calgary. These two have decided to meet Kever and me at a shopping mall at 5:30 in the morning, so there's not a minute to lose. It's still dark. Kever is just pouring our tea into a big thermos and I'm getting our equipment together.

Sharptail grouse equipment: binoculars, camera, sunglasses, warm clothes, tea, cookies.

Smitty and Jill are waiting in the parking lot at the Westgate Shopping Mall. Smitty stands outside the car; Jill sits inside. The only other traffic is the odd bit of lowlife going home from all-night revels. A big guy on a hog cruises up to our cars and the vehicles of several other birders, checks us all out and takes off with an explosive sound that celebrates man's freedom from mufflers on the streets of Saskatoon. No drug deals here, perhaps he is thinking.

Smitty gets out of his car and approaches and beckons me over for a conference. "Hi," he whispers. "Are you still planning to double up with us?"

"Yes. Of course. Why?"

Smitty is still whispering. "Well, the thing you should know is that, um, in her present condition, Jill doesn't actually start talking till about nine or ten o'clock."

"You mean she has the pregnant-type morning grumps?"

"Yeah! That's it!"

Smitty seems grateful.

"So, don't expect that if you talk to her that she'll . . . answer you back?"

"Right. I'll tell Kever."

When the leader of the birding group, Jim Wedgwood, arrives, we all double up, four to a car, to minimize the number of vehicles out on the prairie. Then we head out west in a caravan of seven or eight cars. Smitty drives an Oldsmobile Delta 88 Royal Brougham that sails like a sampan along the highway and takes the dips and winds like rollers and swells. A very comfortable old car. It makes bucket seats and economy-sized automobiles seem somehow uncivilized.

"So," says Smitty, "Jill would like to know why we are gathered so early."

"We have no idea," says Kever. "Maybe because it's still dark, they let you approach them."

Jill whispers something to Smitty.

"Jill would like to know what happens if we don't see where we're going and drive right over their nests."

"No sweat," I tell them. "There's no nesting in the dance area. Mostly it's dancing males and a few hens standing by. Maybe the nesting hens are off in the bush somewhere."

All Kever and I know for sure is that this is the best time of the year to watch the sharptails dance, and only one man seems to know where they can best be watched. Jim Wedgwood is a retired professor of ornithology and a mainstay of the Saskatoon Natural History Society. He is very keen on anything to do with birding, even at 5:30 A.M.

Wedgwood takes our caravan past Pike Lake and turns into a rolling field of mixed prairie grasses and shrubs. The soil is too sandy for grain. If you were walking in broad daylight, you would find cactus and sage all over this field. We drive behind our leader over a cattle trail until, at last, he extinguishes his headlights and comes to a stop. It is still completely dark in the west, but over the high ground and willow copses a faint light begins to seep. Far to the southeast a rim of light has appeared, which means that the sun will rise within the hour.

Once again Jill whispers in Smitty's ear.

"Jill would like to know why we are stopping."

We strain to see something that might look like a bird on the ground. Nothing. Wedgwood moves forward slowly for about twenty yards and once again stops his car. We are right behind him and climbing out of a shallow dip in the trail. When we ease up to the high ground, I can see, perhaps 40 yards ahead, what appears to be seven or eight white handkerchiefs flapping in the wind.

But there *is* no wind.

"Guys!"

"Where?" says Kever.

"Where?" says Smitty.

I point to the hankies, now at least a dozen of them, and they are not all white, none of them are white, just their undersides. And just like that, they reconstitute themselves as birds. Birds as large as pullets. At first they seem to be the colour of dust, but as Smitty brings his vehicle up next to Wedgwood's car and turns off his engine, we can see that the grouse are a great deal more than the colour of dust. The feathers on their underparts are shaped like dappled brownish scales on a downy white background. They are darker on top, with a range of browns, black and grey, and unlike the prairie chickens that used to inhabit this area, the birds have a sharp tail, a smaller version of the tail on a hen pheasant.

By my count there are fifteen dancers, all of them cocks. Three or four hens stand unimpressed at the edge of the dancing grounds like teenage girls at a small-town hockey game. The cocks cackle and coo, rattle their quills and inflate their neck sacks. Sometimes the cooing becomes a louder booming sound that can be heard a mile away.

As the sun nears the rim of the prairie we can see just how colourful these cocks really are. When inflated, their neck sacs are a shameless purple, like snap-on male egos. Over their eyes are yellow combs that seem to flare and expand during the dance.

"My God!" whispers Smitty.

It's like a signal. The cocks begin to circle on the dancing ground, testing the edges of their territory, venturing onto the edges of their rivals' territory. The theory goes that the cock who can maintain the choicest territory in the centre of the dancing grounds will maintain his place on the hierarchy and perhaps also have his choice of hens. By now, towards the end of April, some of these hens are already on the nests, which are usually within a mile or so of the dancing grounds but never *on* the dancing grounds. This field of jousting has about as much to do with actual conception as a prizefighting ring.

Have you ever watched a fighter during the last few minutes leading up to a boxing match? He comes up to the ring with his entourage and slowly climbs through the ropes like a reigning prince. He checks out the crowd, the ropes, his corner, the laces on his gloves—anything but his opponent. When he paces back and forth, he does so with a bullfighter's contemptuous authority; he creates the illusion that he is used to walking through locked doors without blinking. You can admire him if you want, but you don't mess with him. During the instructions from the referee, he will sometimes look at his opponent and sometimes even try to stare him down. Then the bell goes, the fighters circle cautiously, and a strange, ancient, formalized dance begins. Sometimes they dance apart; sometimes they are locked in stubborn embrace. To a civilized mind, the thought of two warriors *dancing* might seem ludicrous, but the territorial intent is deadly serious and as timeless as Cain and Abel.

You might be tempted, as I am, to see the competition for a divisional belt as an attempt to move up in the pecking order.

There is something deeper than spectacle at a boxing match, something utterly primitive that transcends the smell of dirty money and senseless violence.

And here, on a sagebrush prairie, where the pecking order is more literal than metaphorical, you begin to make the connections. The cocks begin to dance. Their wings are spread out and arched downwards, not flapping, merely displayed as if to show off their pectoral muscles. They stomp and rattle their tails, then zigzag across their territories. A rival will move up and do the same. One of them will cross over into the other's territory. Just when you think you're about to see a cockfight, a violent spectacle, something odd happens—always happens: one of the birds retreats, ushered out by the dominant bird. In fact, they run together, like ballet dancers, mincing across the stage side by side, Baryshnicocks in studied motion. First one contending pair then another. You can almost hear Tchaikovsky's score for the war between the toy soldiers and the rats.

There is scarcely a drop of blood or a lost feather to be seen. The reason for this ritualized violence is, I guess, fairly obvious. The sharptails can't afford to give way to their impulse to fight as trained cocks are supposed to do, because if they did, they would kill each other. And unlike some more fortunate species on this planet, such as human beings, the sharptails are beginning to disappear from the face of the earth. Their habitat in Saskatchewan is being destroyed by farmers and by settlements, sometimes for the most baffling of motives. Dancing grounds are being ploughed under, planted, sprayed with chemicals, allowed to erode and then in some cases abandoned.

By now I've counted twenty male birds, and it suddenly hits me: they are doing what many of the Native dancers up here call the Prairie Chicken Dance. The spins, the hunkering down, the short runs, the flutter jumps with feathered arms arched down. One of the oldest dances in all of North America.

"My God!" cries Jill, her first public utterance of the morning.

If you become a tourist in Saskatchewan, you might not be lucky enough to see this spectacle, which stretches from late winter to late spring. There are not many guides who are willing to go out, as Wedgwood has done, free of charge, and find a good lek that people can view.

Watching Native troupes do the Prairie Chicken Dance is a bit easier to arrange. If you get this chance to see the Cree or the Sioux dancers, you must grab it. The Native dancers are so good at reminding us—much better than pro boxers have ever done—of the profound connections between the natural and the human world. Watching this dance makes you wonder if the human species will evolve as far as the sharptail grouse and learn to ritualize its violence all across the globe. Perhaps on that day we'll all join the dance.

THE PLACE WHERE THE X IS

THERE'S A STRETCH of the year when time goes by too fast to be marked. If I could guess, I'd say that it starts about the end of April, when we dig the garden, and begins to slow down in July, when the back yard is in full bloom.

On the first sunny day in May the light is so intense I feel like a mole in a tanning salon.

The leap from April into May is saturnalian.

It's almost time to head up north to Little Bear Lake and Narrow Hills Park. It's just about time, friends, one and all, to go fly-fishing.

All through March and April I have purchased everything I might need for the fly-fishing season. New fly lines, wet and dry. New leaders for my fly lines, new tippets for my leaders, new flies for my tippets, wet and dry. I've practically memorized every trout stats column in my latest "Fish Facts," bought my fishing licence, booked off a week, lined up my fishing buddies, phoned the Mogensons (who run Little Bear Lake Lodge) about a dozen times. Perhaps even more than a dozen times.

"How's the, ah, ice situation, Alice?"

"Frozen tight as a drum, Dave."

"How're things looking up there, Ken?"

"Little early yet, Dave."

"How's the, ah, ice situation, Alice?"

"Not much to report, Dave."

"How goes the battle, Ken?"

"Try ringin us next week, Dave."

"How's the, ah, ice situation, Alice?"

"Oh, Dave, we had us a real blizzard yesterday. You might just ring us up a little closer to opening day."

"Things still frozen up there, Ken?"

"Well, Dave, we've had a small bit of melting around the cabin, but the lakes are all froze up yet."

"Oh, Alice, by the way, how's—"

"Pretty much the same, Dave."

"Say, Ken, while I'm talking to you up there, what's the—"

"We'll call you, Dave. Okay?"

"How's—"

"Froze up."

"Still—"

"Yup."

But something happens. It always does. The sun performs its patient work on the deep drifts of snow that lie heavy in the northern woods and the pale blue carapaces that cover every northern lake until the second week of May. And fishing comes to those who wait.

I have only a few fishing buddies who approach my certifiable state of obsession. Warren Cariou is the most obsessed and the most athletic, the Wayne Gretzky of Saskatchewan fly-fishing. He has the fine co-ordination of a Swiss watch. He is focussed and he's deadly.

Bill Robertson is the very embodiment of determination. He will stop short of nothing to get the trout in the net. This includes death-defying dives in scrotumtightening waters that would discourage even otters, beavers and muskrats.

Bob Calder is more of a Clint Eastwood character. He wears dark glasses, an ancient black flotation jacket and a wide-brimmed Tilly hat, and he casts for trout through the mystical smoke of a Ritmeester cigar, which he uses for camouflage as well as to fend off mosquitoes. He hauls the trout in, releases them and moves on like smoke into the muskeg. You can almost hear that theme music from *The Good, the Bad, and the Ugly,* the refrain that sounds like a calling loon.

Doug Elsasser is a compact, sturdy guy who looks like Bruce Springsteen. Rumour has it that he gathers leeches and uses them for bait, but who am I to judge the moral worth of a man who can carry a big canoe on his shoulders and slap mosquitoes *at the same time?* You don't impugn the worth of the man who carries the canoe.

Kever is a combination of Meryl Streep in *River Wild* and Annie Oakley. She goes it alone with the belly boat, drifting to her own music among the trout like a synchronized swimmer until the trout begin to feed beneath her inner tube. She picks them off one by one. Some of her casts take fish less than a canoe's length away from her flippers.

We eat well in May.

More than half of Saskatchewan is northern forest and Precambrian rock. This combination makes for thousands of northern lakes full of fish, many so far back in the bush that they haven't even been named or seen a floatplane. Up around Little Bear and all through Narrow Hills Park there are clusters of blue and green ponds so clear you can see to the bottom a hundred yards from shore. The water is clear as a Jasper lake and packed with nutrients. Freshwater shrimp, boatmen, caddis nymphs, midges, stickleback minnows, dragonfly nymphs, ciscoes, mosquito larvae, water beetles, leeches, snails, frogs, mayfly nymphs. The trout grow fast and taste even better than wild chinooks and coho. The trout meat is moister and sweeter. The idea is to catch enough for the next day's breakfast or for supper and let the rest go.

You clean the little ones, dip them in egg and flour, line their bellies with fresh dill and lime, and fry them in butter. Add a dash of pepper.

The big ones are nice for baking or barbecuing. I love to stuff the biggest brookies and brown trout in the spring and the even bigger rainbows in the fall. That way I avoid messing with spawning fish, since most rainbows are spring spawners, most brown trout spawn in September, and most brook trout spawn in October and November.

My stuffing for large trout is from an old family recipe. It's made of sautéed onions, celery and wild mushrooms, with dried bread crumbs, pepper and fresh basil. Make more than you need to stuff the cavity of the big trout and pack the extra stuffing just outside the cavity. No need for skewers to close the cavity; just wrap the stuffed trout and the overflow stuffing in one or two sheets of foil and stick it on the barbecue or into the oven. Barbecue about ten minutes for each side or bake for up to an hour at 350°F. The trout bakes in its own abundant fat and juice. It's done when you can sink a paring knife or a skewer easily into the side of the fish, through the thickest flesh, right down to the backbone.

Two years ago, Calder caught a rainbow that fed six people. Last year, Cariou caught a brown that fed everyone in camp. Last year I caught a brook trout that was twenty-five inches long. I couldn't wrap its body in one piece of foil, so I had to double up. A few years ago, Kever caught an eight-pound rainbow that towed her belly boat. We have all lost trout so mighty that we still mumble into our pillows about broken lines and boat-high leaps. Most of the time, however, we are lucky to catch a few good trout and are content to release most of our day's catch. Again, because of spawning, we tend to release more rainbows in the spring and more browns and brooks in the fall.

I talk about these three species as if you knew them as intimately as I. A few introductions are in order. The most exciting fighters are the rainbows. Not only do they grow larger than the other two species, but they are olympic runners and jumpers. They feel like chinook or coho salmon, except their runs are generally shorter and their mighty leaps more frequent. Never look for subtlety in a rainbow. Look for spectacle.

The brown trout is by far the hardest to catch. Not only is the brown a powerful swimmer, but it knows every snag in the stream.

It is wily and subtle. Browns are not native to this part of the world; they are native Europeans. They used to thrive in the small clear streams of northern Europe and the British Isles. They must have learned their cautious, nocturnal habits from these clear streams where a trout in the open is vulnerable to birds, otters and anglers. They've brought this wiliness over here. Only the fly-fisher has a realistic hope of catching one or two.

The brook trout is perhaps my favourite. It is the smallest of the three. Landing a two-pounder is a real occasion. A real good brookie is more often about fourteen inches long and weighs less than a pound and a half. Brookies are wonderful to eat and wonderful to catch. But their greatest appeal is surely their extraordinary beauty. They vary a great deal, but the brookies we catch up north usually have olive-green backs with a distinct pattern of wormlike markings called vermiculations. Their sides are sometimes golden, sometimes pale green, with bright pink spots surrounded with bluish halos. When the spawning is about to begin, the flanks of the male brookies take on a brilliant orange hue. Their fins are red, edged with black and creamy slashes.

Perhaps some day our brookies should go on a stamp. Canada has the finest brook trout fishing in the world.

My friends and I have evolved a method of locating hot spots that depends a lot on teamwork. There are about thirty good lakes and several good streams in the vicinity of Narrow Hills Park. Almost never do these waters all yield good trout at the same time. The feeding activity can vary from lake to lake, depending on what the temperature of the water is, how much food is available, whether some fish are spawning or how well the fish have survived the long winter. On our first day out, we tend to split up, fish for a while in a likely spot or two and then pool our information at the end of the day.

Sometimes it might take us two full days of trial-and-error fishing until we hit the right spot. In the fall of 1992, we were in an unusual bind. We had invited a CBC crew from the radio program *IDEAS* to do a piece on our fishing trips. It was unusually cold, we were all freezing half to death, and after two days of advance scouting we hadn't caught a single fish. What made this state of affairs doubly bad was that the recording crew was insisting that we do our interviews while catching fish!

Just before the CBC crew was to arrive, Kever took a walk down by the shores of Sealey Lake. She found an elderly woman there scanning the waters for her husband, who was trying his luck at the far end in a motorboat. Kever confessed to the woman that we hadn't caught a single fish and that we needed to show the CBC crew *some* signs of life. The woman looked at Kever for a moment and said, "Why not try over there?" She was pointing northeast at a small bay surrounded by bush. "Come on," she said. "I'll show you." She took Kever along a path over a rocky ridge and through some dense berry bushes. It looked like an ideal spot to encounter a bear. But when they arrived once more at the shoreline, Kever spotted a rising trout. Then another. They were dimpling the water only about twenty feet from shore.

"My husband caught a six-pound rainbow right here last May," said the woman. "And on that same day in May, I caught a four-pound brook trout."

Kever thanked the woman profusely for this information. She returned with her rod and cast into the boiling water. Immediately she had a strike and pulled in a nice foot-long brook trout. She killed the fish, put it into the creel and brought it back to camp.

Maybe I'm overdramatizing things here, but as I remember it, this was the very moment that the CBC crew arrived in their van. Producer Wayne Schmalz called out from the driver's seat, "How's the fishing?"

Kever held up her brook trout and tried to look casual. "Not bad," she said.

This turned out to be a prophetic remark. From that moment on, fishing was great.

On one particularly challenging trip in May, a more recent one, we had exhausted ourselves on lakes in which the water was still too cold to promote much insect activity. The fish were there but they were dormant. We had a meeting. We compared all of our findings and "Fish Facts" stats and brought out the maps. There was one lake no one seemed to fish, but reports from the provincial fisheries guys were pretty positive. An abundance of good-sized rainbows and brookies. The lake was hard to get to, it involved some hiking, and going there would mean some pretty heavy lifting of equipment.

But we had Elsasser and a reasonably light seventeen-foot-Grumman canoe. This canoe would seat three of us, a paddler and two anglers. We also had a belly boat for our fourth angler. The idea was that we would all get to trade off with each other. So we all had a pretty heavy load to carry into the bush that morning.

The weather had been brutally cold, but on this particular morning, the sun came up into a windless blue sky.

I am going to call this hike-in lake by its unofficial name. It is The Lake That Cannot Be Named. You have probably guessed why.

We carried rods, lunches in a large cooler, fishing vests and boxes, life jackets, paddles, a belly boat, creel, waders, frog fins and rain gear and followed Elsasser into the woods. To be more precise, we followed our big aluminum canoe into the woods. It seemed to float through the trees like a well-fed shark and did not stop once until it came to the lake it was meant to glide in.

This lake is not much more than a large pond, probably less than a hundred acres. Our arrival was announced by the call of a loon at the near end, and it was answered by her mate at the far end. On all sides the lake was sheltered by high-rising cliffs and gentle slopes. If a wind came up, there would be no danger of squalls. The shallows were pale green, the deeper water emerald and the deepest holes sapphire. One by one we clambered down to the little beach where Doug had placed the canoe. The water off the far shore was dimpled with rising trout.

We began at once to tie on flies. When you have puffed your way along a trail that leads to the fly-fisher's version of Treasure Island and finally reached the place where the *X* is, you discover that the simple job of tying on a fly is fraught with difficulties. The idea is to turn away from the lake and try to think of anything but trout. Think of potatoes or the label on a tin of Ovaltine, think of people you owe money to, or try to recall the exact wording for the French version of "O Canada." Anything to get your mind off the feeding frenzy of several thousand plump silver torpedos about to make your day.

Judging from the language unleashed behind me at leaders and hooks and snags, I would have to say, with embarrassment, that my friends have failed to master this simple meditation.

Kever's fly rod was finally ready. On the end of her line she had a fly that imitates a large black leech. She pulled on her set of neo-prene waders. Then she sat down on a log and pulled on a huge set of frog fins. For added security and buoyancy, she put on her life jacket, and then she stepped into her belly boat. This is a fancy inner tube equipped with many pockets for equipment and lunch and a harness affair that she stepped through. Then, holding onto her big tube, she moved on flippers backwards into the water.

Ungainly and waddling on shore, she was positively balletic on water. Away she went, flippers churning the silt, her body sus-pended in cool water, her fly rod aloft, elbows leaning at ease on the belly boat. Periodically she checked her progress by turning around to zero in on where the trout were rising. She had to do this because in a belly boat you can only move forward by going backwards.

Finally the three guys were ready. I paddled us out onto the lake and headed for the deeper water. They began the day by trolling backswimmers and muddler minnows. The former is a wet fly with two arms that imitate the "oars" of a water beetle sometimes called a boatman. The latter is a fly originally tied by Ontarians to catch brook trout in the fabled Nipegon River. Trolling flies is a good way of testing the waters. You simply point your rod tip in the direction of your submerged fly, keep the tip down, and wait for something to hit that is strong enough to pull your arm off.

It didn't take long.

"I've got one," said Calder in a whisper.

I'm not sure why he whispered. It sounded as though he were trying not to publicize his good luck to all the anglers—who might have been hiding by the dozens in the bushes, scanning our progress with binoculars and electronic devices. But we were all alone on that small lake.

Calder's rainbow grabbed his fly and took off for the middle of the lake. His reel was buzzing like a chain saw, and then the line went limp.

"Damn."

He slumped over in the canoe and was about to reach for a cigar when his fish leapt right beside us a good three feet out of the water. It was a very big rainbow.

I was heard to give the following sage advice. "Gone not on your lift it! Lift it! He's fish on your! Calder! No! Yes! Bob! In! Reel hold your up! Tip! Rod! A fish!"

Kever looked over from her belly boat perhaps to see if I were suffering from a stroke or dyslexia. She too was landing a fish.

Elsasser kept his cool, reeled in his line and grabbed the landing net.

Calder's rainbow took a second long run, and once again the reel buzzed. Then his fish repeated his little trick of turning around and coming back at the boat like Moby Dick about to ram the *Pequod*. Calder reeled in as fast as he could, but not fast enough. Again, the rainbow sailed out into the sky and re-entered with a histrionic splash. And off he went, gone. Escaped.

Well, no, just free on a slack line, and this time Calder was wise to his fish. He reeled in and felt the surge of another mighty run.

Kever's fish was a brookie, a deep fighter by the looks of things. She played it, led it into the net, released it, and before Calder had managed to tire his big rainbow, she had a second fish on.

Looking a bit wrung out, Calder finally led his fish into the net and handed it over to Elsasser, and Elsasser brained it with his priest. When the rainbow was safely in the bottom of the boat, Calder finally lost his composure. He offered up the angler's equivalent of a loud hosanna: "Yeeeeeeeeeeehaaaw!"

The loons looked up from their lovemaking.

We paddled past Kever, and Calder held his fish up. It had obviously finished its spawning. This rainbow was as silver as silver and had a faint purple stripe down both sides. It was almost twenty-one inches long. Kever responded by raising up her second brookie of the day, a plump fifteen-inch beauty. (This brook trout was to feed all four of us that night.) I took our canoe through a narrow gap and into the smaller half of the lake, the northern half, so well shaded that the water is a very deep emerald, the air cool and piny. Here the surface was virtually without a riffle and sent back unbroken reflections of the high cliffs and shaggy spruce. Near shore in deep water next to some steep mossy boulders, a rise on or near to the surface. Another rise. A bevy of rises. We were all afloat on a lyric dream of emerald and rising trout.

"Got one."

It was Elsasser's turn now, another big rainbow. This one was loath to jump and streaked for the centre of our bay. It seemed even stronger in its runs than Calder's mighty fish of half an hour ago.

Kever paddled behind us and into the bay. She began to cast. Calder brought in his line, but before he could lift his fly from the water, his fly rod plunged down for the bottom like a diviner's willow.

"My God, I've got another big one!"

By now, no one was whispering. Chaos was about to take over. I paddled hard for the centre of the bay. I needed to keep us all in deep water so that the fish couldn't dive down into the snags and snap our lines.

"Kever!" I cried. "We need you over here to help with the landing!"

"Okay."

Kever wound in her line. She hadn't recovered twenty feet when she was fast to a burly diver of her own. She looked my way, shrugged.

"Sorry," she said.

Calder's rainbow dove under Elsasser's line and soared out of the water. A chunky three-pounder. It swam back the way it came and the lines crossed. At last Elsasser's fish, a much bigger, darker rainbow, breached beside the boat, drawing a host of exclamations and gasps.

Kever's fish was a brookie. It seemed to be curious about the melee near our canoe. It ploughed over in our direction.

"No!" I cried.

"I can't stop it!" yelled Kever.

"Well, do something!"

Kever lifted her rod tip, palmed her reel and put on all the pressure she could risk, and at last her brookie came back towards her belly boat. It began to sulk in the deep water below her and would not move.

"Thank God," said Calder.

"Close one," said Doug.

Then his rainbow took off once more and broke the surface on the run. It seemed to get bigger with each new leap. It had become so badly tangled with Calder's line that Calder must have felt as though he were landing two rainbows.

"Something has to give," he said grimly.

It did.

Doug Elsasser's line snapped, and he was left with a memory of the biggest rainbow he had ever seen. Open-mouthed and mumbling, he wound in his line. Now hookless, it came free from Calder's fly line, and Bob brought in his three-pound rainbow. He smiled over at Kever as she held up her brook trout, the fat twin of her second brookie. If ever an opera is written about fly-fishing, there would have to be that inevitable exchange between anglers over the rise and fall of Fortune's Wheel. (The magic wheel, in angler's jargon, is the fishing reel.) Such an aria would give voice to Calder's triumph and Kever's exultation and Elsasser's whispered imprecations at an unkind fate. I've gotta see Placido Domingo in Elsasser's role. He's got that tragic range.

It doesn't happen very often, but on that day we simply lost count. We lost some big fish, we regained our composure, caught and released our limit, and emerged from the lake and the trail by late afternoon. We were exhausted, but what an amazing day. The hiking in, the shore lunch, the fishing—it all went by so fast we could only gush in wonderment all the way back to the camp.

The day I've been writing about was so entirely perfect it deserves to be set aside as a national holiday. May 22, 1993. The next day the fishing was just as good, the weather even warmer. The water beetles gathered beneath the cooler shadows of the fallen trees, and even the frogs moved languidly around the edges of the pond. Something was in the air.

We drove back to Saskatoon on May 24, and the whole week's accumulated heat seemed to warm everything up, even the depths of parkland soil so long frozen during five months of winter. The heat seemed to rise in great waves off the pastures, newly seeded fields and aspen groves. In the city, legions of songbirds gathered beneath the cool gloom of the trees. When we left Saskatoon, the buds were on the trees in a sweet profusion. Now they were in full leaf. Several days before the end of May, summer had arrived.

PART THREE

Summer

Nature's Rejection Slip

On the evening of the summer solstice, Kever likes to drive Will and me out to the Dairy Queen on 8th Street. She waits until about 10:00, when the sun is still riding on the western horizon. We're always impressed at the amount of daylight. The Dairy Queen on 8th is so small it's a sort of glorified kiosk. You order from one of the twin wickets and take your treat over to the benches beside the building. At this time of year there's always a lineup.

This is how it was on the first day of summer when Kever arrived from Arizona in 1975. She watched it from the window of her motel, this lineup of eager Saskatonians, several generations of them, but mostly kids with their parents. Where she came from, the kids would be in bed, and so would most of the adults. Where she came from it would have been *dark* out. For reasons she may never fully explain to her own satisfaction, she sensed that in 1975 she had arrived in a different country.

I'd never seen anything unusual about a bunch of families lining up for a late-night milkshake.

I asked her, "What did you *say* when you saw these people eating ice cream till past midnight?"

"I think I said something like, 'Is that ever neat.'"

June flies by so fast that it demands to be appreciated from its very first day. All that dazzling light diminished but not entirely extinguished by brief nights. All that warmth on the skin. The best week in June is the first week, because as the sun warms the earth and the sloughs and our bodies, there are scarcely any mosquitoes.

There are, however, other hatches in June. Mayflies, for example, and stoneflies. I suppose you see where this thing is going.

This is going down to the southwest corner of the province to the Cypress Hills, and yes, for God's sake, bring your fly rod and your waders.

Hurry. There is not one second to waste. You dally one tiny bit and June is gone and so is youth and hope and and and . . . Anyway, hurry. The stoneflies are hatching and the trout are rising and—

But remember, if you hurry, you will miss the great gifts of this month, so slow down, yes, that's it, slow right down, breathe in the alfalfa breath of June and do whatever you do to retard the merciless march of time and do what I've never managed to do: make June eternal.

But for God's sake, hurry.

The Cypress Hills, Wallace Stegner tells us in his classic *Wolf Willow,* are the highest point in Canada between Labrador and the Rockies.

> *Everything about them is special, and everything special about them is explained by the accident of elevation. Their topography, their climate, their plants and animals, their peculiar geographical and zoological lags and survivals, even their human history, are what they are because this uplift has been pushed a thousand to fifteen hundred feet above the plains that apron it. . . . Geologically [the Hills] are an anomaly, and display in their higher strata rocks that were elsewhere planed away by the ice. Biologically they preserve Rocky Mountain plants and animals far out into the Plains, and southern species far into the north. Wild West longer than anywhere else, last home of buffalo and grizzlies, last sanctuary for the Plains hostiles, last survival of the open-range cattle industry . . . this country saved each stage of the Plains frontier long past its appointed time, and carried 19th-century patterns of culture well into the 20th. All because the Hills are a thousand feet higher than the rest of Saskatchewan.*

Driving from the north, when you get past Gull Lake and look south, you get your first real good view of the Cypress Hills proper. They rise high and massive, muted purple, like the first sight of land on a voyage west. You'd almost think that there is some mistake. Perhaps you have wandered into Montana. Most people will be tempted to continue southwest to Maple Creek and then turn south to enter the park. This is the efficient route.

If you have time, however, and you like to have your breath taken away by the scenery, and if you want to see pronghorn antelope, whitetails and badgers, and do some birding and that sort of thing, drive south from Tompkins on a small gravel highway called 633. This joins up with Highway 614 to the west and takes you south to a jewel of a town known as Eastend. Together these dusty little roads are among the prettiest drives in all of Western Canada. They can't vie with the Banff-Jasper Highway for spectacle, but, seen another way, the Banff-Jasper Highway can't vie with these little roads for intimacy and subtlety and bucolic appeal.

This antelope haven of ridges and meadows, knolls and hollows, is the rangeland. It is distinguished by white clay hills filled with glacial moraine deposits in the coulees and hollows and on the small plateaus. Between the slopes and through the gullies flow some very pretty little streams, some too small to be of interest to anglers, others just deep and wide enough to make you want to slow down and do some serious water gazing. Nowhere else on the Canadian prairie can you ogle such streams.

Our destination is the Spring Valley Guest Ranch near Ravenscrag. Jim Saville runs a bed and breakfast there in a big old house that he had to move—from Irvine, Alberta, by semi-trailer—into the valley. I don't know exactly how he did it. This is a large, classy 1800-square-foot house with a big third-floor attic. It was built in 1913 and weighed in at well over seventy-five tons.

Jim's house and barn lie adjacent to his parents' big spread where Jim grew up. It helps that Jim was a ranch kid, and helps even more that he has a gracious and welcoming way about him that does credit to country hospitality. This is my absolute favourite B & B in all of Western Canada. In announcing these facts, my motives are completely altruistic. Sometimes, when a traveller believes that he has found paradise, he can't help telling the world about it. Each time Kever and I take our binocs and fly rods to Jim's rangeland B & B, we return with a renewed conviction that yes, we have seen something down there as close to perfect as a weary traveller is ever likely to find.

Let me distinguish here between traveller and tourist. The tourists will never discover Jim's B & B, except perhaps by accident. The tourists go for the high-profile stuff. The Calgary Stampede, the Olympics, the World's Fair, the Grey Cup. The tourists can afford to stay in the most expensive motels. They can stay in places almost identical to the ones in their own home town. Always a little suspicious of people they don't know, the tourists play it by the book, which in most cases is the tourist brochure. Tourists can go to New York and do it up in such a way that they return with all illusions intact. *The Bronx? We didn't go to the Bronx. No one goes to the Bronx.*

The traveller, however, avoids major highways, expensive motels, huge crowds, Banff in July and other officially sanctioned tourist spectacles. Travellers avoid tourists. They prefer to read books about a destination rather than brochures. They want to learn something about the new place and return with as few illusions as possible. They seek to be enlarged by their experience of the place. At worst, the tourist tends to be a money snob. At worst, the traveller is just as likely to be a human growth snob.

Jim Saville isn't the type to warble about human growth. He's too busy cooking, fixing things and showing his guests a good time. On Saturday nights he opens up the top floor of his barn for country dancing. It's a classic old red barn, with animals and poultry on the main floor and dancers in the loft. In fact, Jim teaches country dances to the ranching folk from the surrounding district and to his guests at the house. There's a cultural influence for you; country dancing flourishes in Jim Saville's area. When he has the time, Jim also takes you up onto the table land to explore the surrounding valleys by horseback. Once he led us along a creek to a hillside where the spring water that fed the creek tumbled out of the side of the hill like some sort of Biblical miracle. After a long hike, there is rarely anything so refreshing as spring water at the source.

Another nice thing about Jim's place is the layout of the B & B itself. For trout fanatics like me, there is a nicely stocked stream that moves through his back yard. I never keep my trout from here because they are too easily fished out, but I've spent many a happy hour of catch-and-release fishing. (I see myself as the trout's teacher. I educate them about the dangers of fish hooks.)

Just outside the front yard and beyond the barn, Jim has a flock of domestic fowl. Many of these are exotic ducks that Jim keeps as pets. The duck motif is carried on inside the house in every room. He even cooks ducks as part of his supper offerings, but he assures me that none of these morsels are his exotic friends that waddle to and from the trout stream to preen and water each morning. Farther along into the bush, Jim has some Native tepees for the more adventurous campers. During the warmest nights kids can bring their sleeping bags and sleep in the tepees. On colder nights, campers sometimes nurse a small fire inside the tepees to keep out the chill.

When the weather turns stormy, it is dramatically stormy, and you run up to the ridges to watch the sky wage war upon and then replenish the Earth.

In June of 1995, I drove down to Saville's place with Will and Kever. As usual, there were a number of things we wanted to do. Kever wanted to do some country dancing and see the excavation of T Rex, one of the world's best-preserved examples of a *Tyrannosaurus*. I wanted to attend a festival of cowboy poetry, and Will wanted to hike into the hills and see the spring, mentioned above, that comes tumbling out of the side of the hill.

I had another reason, of course. *Toujours, cherchez le poisson*, I suppose you could say.

A certain brown trout. I had seen this one before but I'd never been able to catch it. The quest for this brown trout had become an adventure of mythic proportions. So keen had I become to catch it, I began to wonder if anyone alive, even Kever, could appreciate the urgency of my mission. I began a campaign of dissimulation, playing down the moment when I would creep to my special spot for my special adversary.

Adversary is the word. The big brown had become a Moriarty to my Holmes. Even for me this is a *bit* unusual.

It all started in June of 1993. I wanted to fish a creek in the Centre Block of Cypress Hills Provincial Park. I mention this because I often have better luck outside the park in the surrounding hills. But this fine day I had driven alone from Jim's place near Ravenscrag to the parking lot at Loch Leven. I did some gabbing there with a conservation officer. I told him about the creek I wanted to fish and where I intended to walk. I also told him that this time I hoped to find some of those old browns rumoured to be still in the creek.

"Yes," he said, one brown trout lover to another. "There's still some old spawners in there. That's why the smaller ones keep showing up."

Old spawners. How that phrase makes my heart leap. The older a brown trout gets, the bigger it gets. I must have gawked at this fellow as though I were Jim Hawkins and he were Long John Silver. Anglers in the vicinity will no doubt recognize the spot, because (although I've never met another angler when I was there), I've always found some telltale waderprints from other fly-fishers. This used to be primarily a brown trout stream, but for some reason, the creek was now full of brook trout and the occasional rainbow. I began to tell the man where I intended to hike to.

"You cross the stile, walk down through the pasture, and go upstream?" the conservation officer said.

"Yes, don't you?"

"Well, yeah, everybody goes upstream," said the man. He seemed to hesitate, as though he knew something and was wondering if he should risk imparting it to me.

"Is there anything to be had downstream?" I said. This was my second trip to this water, but I hadn't tried the downstream stretch.

"Well," said the man, "you mind doin a little bushwhackin?"

I bought some snacks and then drove a small road to a heavily wooded, gentle stretch of hills. It was a hot windless evening, and the pale dust behind my car just hung there, suspended, like pollen. I parked my car at the stile beside a large, sparsely wooded pasture. I hiked downhill for several hundred yards and came to my stream. I looked upstream along the streamside path I had previously followed, and I was tempted to follow it again. There were certain guarantees up there, a good supply of brookies that ran up to fourteen inches and enough larger rainbows to make it interesting.

Then I looked downstream. Immediately I remembered why I hadn't previously chosen to walk it. The stream virtually disappeared into a huge tangle of willows and dogwood, cattails and rushes, and all manner of swampy things to snag my fly. As I walked down to the edge of the tangle, I wondered if I shouldn't either give up on the whole idea or walk a mile or two downstream and try the waters way below the spot my friend the conservation officer had mentioned.

I began looking into this marshy mess of thickets for telltale signs of anglers. They always manage to wear a path to their favourite spots. Sometimes the careless ones will leave some trash. It's a dead giveaway. But this time, as I ambled down parallel to the big tangle of brush and weeds, I could find nothing. I tried the other side of the creek, but it was almost unapproachable. For one thing, it was too muskegy. My waders began to sink down into the bog surrounding the creek. I returned to my original side of the creek, the approximate place where I was told to begin. All I could see was a game trail leading through some buffalo berry bushes. The thorns on these bushes are formidable. But there was this game trail, narrow and no more than knee high beneath a jungle of thorns, a trail I imagined only beavers or foxes might use. I got down on my hands and knees and began to crawl towards the sound of the stream.

If you're ever searching for your lost sense of creaturehood, this is a pretty good way to begin. You must small yourself down for the task. Remove all your bulky clothes, including your waders, and carry or drag them all with you. If you wear your waders through a patch of buffalo berry, they will be torn and spring a dozen leaks.

Down low you begin to resemble a creature, perhaps a cougar dragging a carcass to its den or a beaver with a mouthful of willow branches. Humility? I could have cornered the market.

As I crawled past the thorniest stretch, the path got wetter but easier. After a while I was able to crouch and then to stand. Was I following in the path of a cunning and solitary angler? One look at the ground in front of me gave me my answer: a plastic margarine container filled with mud. It could be only one thing. Worms!

I struggled forward and found myself at streamside by an old beaver house. The trick was to climb up onto the rubble of this abandoned lair and cast into the stream.

And what lovely water it was. To my right there was a beaver dam, still maintained with fresh cuttings. The water trickled and flowed over and around this dam into a lower pool. To my left, the stream wound its way slowly and enticingly into the pond formed by the dam and flowed well out from my station on the shore into a stretch of deep open water about ten yards wide and at least twenty yards long.

Glurp! went a feeding trout by the reeds at the near edge of the pond.

Glurp! went another in the lily pads on the other side.

They were rising for stoneflies on the surface of the pond and all along the banks of the creek, and they rose with heartstopping authority. I couldn't quite see these trout. The reflection from the sun and the dark bottom prevented me, but the size of the rings they created and the size of their heads and dorsals left very little to the imagination. Some of these babies were big.

I assembled my rod and fumbled a stonefly imitation onto my leader. There was very little room for a backcast, so I heaved my line more up than back and sent my fly towards the incoming stream. It drifted about six feet my way and then *schlup!* It was gone. I struck back and felt a sort of loglike resistance to my strike. Something big and long and golden brown gleamed for an instant in the water beneath my perch, and then with a violent lurch it took off and snapped my leader.

The thing that bothered me was how easily the line snapped, as though it were a cobweb and not a sturdy piece of five-pound monofilament.

That was it. No more rising. No more fish. They were all spooked and fled to other holes or sulked on the bottom. It's the way of a brown trout to be wily in this manner. Except at night. But this was early evening. Trembling all the way down to my shins, I crawled back out of the thicket.

I returned in June of '94 and saw the occasional rise from what looked to be very large fish, but I couldn't get one to go for my fly. At last I landed a brown trout a bit more than sixteen inches long, a very good fish, but not nearly as big as the one that had broken my leader. I discovered something in the stomach of this trout that made the entire process of crawling through thorns and thickets worthwhile: a decomposing water shrew. It was six inches long.

I am an incurably forensic fisherman. I cannot wait to get my fingers into a fish's stomach and begin to sort through the guck. This is not a perversion. At least it is not *merely* a perversion. It's a necessity. If you want to throw a fly to a willing fish, you have to know what's on its menu. In June, for example, your autopsy will yield an abundance of stonefly nymphs or emerging stoneflies. But when a large marauding brown is *really* hungry, well, it gets voracious.

I rediscovered this fact over the winter. Warren Cariou sent me some advice. I read up on brown trout. It all pointed to the same scenario. Fish at twilight or later, as long as there's enough light in the sky to see what you're doing. Use a mouse, vole or shrew imitation. Go for the trout as though you were a hunter, which is to say, stalk it and try for the perfect cast. After a tussle with a big brown in a small beaver pond, there won't be any second chances. Use a shorter rod (for easier casting) and a stouter leader.

I spent the winter of 1994–95 like a recently defeated heavyweight with a return match in his contract. I plotted strategy. First the rod, a sturdy little seven-footer. Then the leader, a size 1x that could pull in a good-sized salmon. And then the fly. None of my fly-tying buddies could imagine how to imitate a small mammal, but in a store in Vancouver given over to the pleasures of bass and pike fishing, I found it. My fly was tied on a huge hook with a monofilament weed guard. It was made almost entirely of deer hair. This was very good, because deer hair is hollow and floats like wood chips. My fly had a long black rubber tail and a sort of buzz cut in the shape of a mouse's head and two plastic beady eyes. I was tempted to buy several, but no, this was a one-shot deal. I would either prevail or I would go down (on all fours) to defeat. Well before June had arrived, I was ready.

Like I say, Kever wanted to see the *Tyrannosaurus* excavation site and Will wanted to do his hike to see the hillside spring, and I was at least pretending to want to see the cowboy poets hold forth in the town of Eastend. Every serious addict needs a ruse.

I couldn't get those big, uncatchable browns out of my mind.

On our way back from the hike with Will, Kever was talking about plate tectonics. She pointed to some strata and referred to an article she had read predicting that a large earthquake would occur on the West Coast.

"Well," she said, "don't you think it's possible?"

There was something in her voice that suggested that I had better answer her question. The problem was, I hadn't the faintest notion what her question was.

"Oh, yes," I said. "Possibly. Probably."

Kever was silent.

"Well, maybe not one hundred per cent," I said.

"Have you heard one word I've been saying in the last hour?"

"What do you mean?"

"You've got that look."

"What look?"

"Like something was bothering you."

"Oh. That look."

"Well?"

"Well what?"

"Is something bothering you?"

Do alcoholics and their spouses have conversations like this? Are their communications wracked by similarly hidden and guilty obsessions? Do they yearn for that moment when at last the truth comes out, the moment when the true tortured self emerges from behind the bloodshot eyes?

"I'm afraid I'm getting these . . . you know."

I made a gesture, familiar to Kever, of waving my hands before my face.

"Oh, my God," she sighed. "You mean—"

"Yes. This time it's brown trout."

Kever and Will agreed to come with me. They dropped me off around 9:00 P.M. There was a bright three-quarter moon on the rise and a lot of remaining light from the sun. Kever and Will would hike upstream and meet me back at the car. If I didn't return, they could come over and give me a shout without their having to crawl through the thorns. This way we could at least keep tabs on one another.

I waved good-bye to Kever and Will at the entrance to my swampy thicket and began to crawl. This time I was aided by a flashlight, and instead of my cumbersome waders, I wore Wellies. At a painfully slow pace, with the small flashlight in my mouth, I crawled forward, hauling my collapsed rod and equipment along with me. I listened for predators. There are precious few in the

Cypress Hills, but at night, the imagination demands such observances.

Had I been in a receptive state, a frame of mind capable of appreciating the natural wonders around me, I would have heard night birds. Chickadees calling or scolding. Night hawks roaring down through swarms of insects. Robins warbling or a late amorous grouse drumming. Before long, I was staring down at the pond and over at the incoming stream. As usual, the beavers were nowhere to be seen and the surface of the pond was unruffled.

A fish rose, and I could just see the rings on the far side of the pond. I assembled my gear to the sound of several more purposeful rises. I tied on the mighty mouse and spat on it for luck. At such a moment a man is one with the youth he used to be. The anticipation is so boundless that there is virtually no difference between the lean and eager fourteen-year-old and the bald and paunchy writer of these words. The first cast of the evening is the very first cast of his angling life.

I began to pull my leader out of the eyes of the rod until I had nine feet of leader and a few feet of line. I hauled out a few metres of line from the reel. Then I began my false cast behind and well above me, back and forth over the pond. I managed to land my mouse right on the grass on the far side of the pond and slowly pulled it off the grass into the lily pads. I could see it rather well in the beams of the flashlight in my mouth. In fact, the small flashlight cast a wide corona over the lily pads. Just as my mouse was hopping from the last of the lily pads to the edge of the water, there was a strange turbulence among the reeds, and that turbulence was heading straight for my mouse. I jerked my killer rodent just a little ways into the water. Something big rolled right over it, and the fly was gone.

What amazes me is that everything happened as it was supposed to. I was floating on a brief illusion of competence. And then, as they say in the fishing mags, all hell broke loose.

Could I really have been floating on a wave of competence? If so, what exactly was it that made me cry out? Because I really did cry out. I said something like "Howy Gweat Gwowling Jeezh," an outcry so unhinged and full of awe that according to Kever it sounded closer to lunacy than profanity. She was alarmed by my cry. Perhaps I should have taken the flashlight out of my mouth.

The trout first ran downstream to my right and to the edge of the dam as if to leap over it and continue downstream and into Montana. Then it reversed its rush and headed upstream right out of the pond.

A voice called out, "David?" The voice of my wife in a state of high alarm.

"Yes?" I spluttered back.

"Are you all right?"

The brown trout had disappeared up the little stream, wound itself around something even more immovable than itself, and then it snapped my super-strength leader.

I removed the flashlight from my mouth. "No," I said.

"What's wrong?" cried Kever.

"I just lost the brown trout of the century."

It might have been four pounds. It might have been eight. But it was so much bigger than any brown trout I had ever landed, it hardly matters how big the fish was. All I know is what happened as I stood on top of my old beaver house, my rod cast aside, the flashlight now in my shaking hand, the trembling beam shining down on the spot where the stream comes murmuring into the beaver pond. Something small came floating my way, a leaf or a bubble. But no, as it floated closer to where I stood, I could see that it was more like a . . . well, like a rejection slip. Or perhaps an admonishment from the spirit that inhabited the creek.

I worked my way down to the water's edge and scooped it up. My mouse fly with a newly straightened hook.

In the Arms of the Tarantula

I won't pretend to be a great lover of July. What hot weather brings to the lives of most people on the prairies I can only begin to appreciate.

I *used* to know, but that was when I lived in Alberta. July meant that school was over and the summer holidays had begun. It meant that our parents would take us out of Edmonton to Lake Wabamun, and for two weeks we would stay at Kapasiwin Beach. There we would live in our bathing suits and scamper through the trees and down the path to the water, where every friend we ever needed would be waiting.

We would rent Old Mr. Edwards's cottage for two weeks. We never once met Old Mr. Edwards, but the word "old" became so attached to his name that after a few years it somehow acquired a capital letter. He was apparently a retired schoolteacher from the little town of Wabamun. His cottage was so old and musty and damp that it seemed more like the corpse of a cottage than a real cottage. Its log footings were no doubt decaying because the cabin kept sagging and sinking lower and lower into the ground.

It was a wonderful cabin. It was located almost forty miles from Edmonton. It slouched on a rise above the lake so close to the beach that we could make it down to the edge of the water in under sixty seconds. You could see schools of striped little perch patrolling the weeds every day. You could catch them with a line, a small silver hook and a hunk of bacon rind. With the help of a flashlight, you could catch toads at night. You could see leeches in the water that would *suck out your blood*. You could catch a big jackfish off the peer and drag it back to the cottage and place it on top of the big block of ice in the ice box with its jaws propped open for Mum to find the next morning. You could time her scream within a few seconds. And she didn't make you clean your own fish because she said you'd just make a mess of it. She was such a good sport.

You could take your BB gun over to Peter Nash's and shoot at just about anything that moved, including Ricky Bemrose. Well, you could do things with your BB gun if you didn't get caught.

Peter Nash had a very dangerous slingshot—not just a forked stick you carved out of the dogwood but a Whamo! slingshot. They were advertised on the backs of comic books, but only Nash actually had the initiative to send away to the States for one.

You could catch garter snakes under the trestle.

Garter snakes. They were small, harmless and common as coyotes. But they were our connection to the jungles of the Amazon and the truly perilous world we yearned for. They were small, black and usually under two feet long, with yellow stripes running the full length of their bodies and bright orange spots on the sides. When you picked them up they sometimes excreted a smelly substance on your hands that lingered for days. All along the tracks you could find their shed skins lying like condoms on the cinders.

Once I asked my brother, "How come the snakes are so cold when it rains and hot when it's sunny?"

"It's obvious," said my brother, in that instructional tone older brothers acquire. "They're cold-blooded. They take on the temperature of the thing they're lying on."

Cold-blooded. No wonder they ate small frogs in such a horrible way. They grabbed them in their mouths and *swallowed them whole.* Very quickly garter snakes became sacred among beasts.

I suppose I'm getting carried away here, but back in the fifties July really was something to get excited about. July was such a wonderfully *unregulated* time of year.

Summer holidays. I can remember what they meant to me and my brother. But now when July comes around and people start to pack their cars for the hot trek out to Paradise, they seem to be joining up with half the tourists in the nation who are *also* heading away from the crowded cities on the road to Paradise. They do so in such numbers that they arrive in equally crowded resorts, and for all I know, their children are almost as unregulated as my brother and I were.

I dunno.

In the first part of June, I can sometimes go outside and find almost no mosquitoes. In the last part of August, the evenings are sometimes wonderfully cool, and the fish begin to bite again. But in July, the heat is so intense that I lurch around the yard like a hippo in search of a wallow.

I like the thunderstorms. But they tend to be rather violent and sometimes they bring hail and destroy the crops.

I like to drink beer in July, but it's probably bad for me.

Once in a while, Kever will think of something to do. An evening of Putt n Bounce, perhaps, or an afternoon of picking saskatoons in late July. Once in a while, Elsasser will come through with a sack of live crawfish and we'll all have a boil. There are some bright souls on our block who drag us downtown to the annual jazz festival, but they know that if I have supper there, I will probably fall asleep in my chair. There are drama festivals all summer long, and I like to attend, but my body always wants to go home or wallow in the river with other hippos. How do normal intelligent people do it? I must be a true northerner. I never seem to come alive until I'm one or two degrees away from hypothermia.

There's one way, though, of getting cool in July without resorting to hippoesque behaviour. I discovered this in the summer of 1985 when Kever and I were getting to know each other. She had persuaded me to go to the Saskatoon Ex, a travelling American carnival. She must have suspected that I would drag my heels on this one, but she primed me for the invitation by telling me that somewhere along the midway, somewhere in the shadow of the double ferris wheel . . .

"Don't keep me in suspense, Kever."

"There's a snake pit."

"You're kidding!"

"It's right here in the paper."

"You mean a *real* snake pit with *real* snakes?"

She showed me the feature in the *Star-Phoenix*. Sure enough, there it was. A tent full of dread-inspiring serpents, some of them so big and long they didn't even need to be poisonous to kill their prey. It was that easy; I was hooked.

What Kever hadn't told me was that she had . . . well . . . a bit of a snake problem. Short of confessing that she was an out-and-out herpephobe, she offered the opinion that they were a bit on the slimy side.

In fact, her plan was to lure me into the midway with the promise of a nice, fulfilling serpent-type experience while she and Will hit the fast rides and the double ferris wheel. She knew already that on the dangerous rides question I was a lost cause. These rides were okay when I was a kid. But somewhere along the way my unquenchable quest for experience became quenchable whenever I found myself being flung through space in a tiny seat surrounded by flying metal bars and vomiting peers.

One warm evening Kever, Will and I drove out in her rusted blue Honda Civic and walked through the turnstiles. A plan began to form, and it certainly wasn't mine. The plan had to do with the togetherness model of contemporary relationships, which involves the sharing of experiences.

The three of us were standing outside the snake pit. Kever sent Will off in the direction of his favourite rides. I thought it might be nice if Kever would accompany me into the snake pit. I was about to show her how brave I was by holding a large snake in my arms. A short pale fellow with a drooping moustache was holding out a reticulated python for the passersby. The python was thirteen feet long.

"Wanna hold my snake?" he said to Kever.

One could tell that no amount of repetition of this, his

favourite line, would diminish its pleasure for him. The snake man had not been blessed with invention.

Instead of bristling at this shamelessly phallic overture, Kever took me aside and said, "How about this?" Kever took in a big breath of warm summer air, the way negotiators must do before a counteroffer. "If you do just one ride with me, I'll hold the snake."

I must have looked down at my sandals or somewhere away from her challenging gaze. Like I say, I had been about to take on the snake myself, partly to show my then girlfriend just how ballsy a guy I could be.

"But if I hold the snake," Kever continued, "you have to promise to stand right there beside me."

"Do I get to choose my ride?" I said. I had the bumper cars in mind.

"Of course," said Kever. "But it has to be a *real* one."

"A real one."

"Yeah. Not one of those kids' things, like the *single* ferris wheel or the *bumper* cars."

"Of course," I said, and began to grow a little clammy.

"What'll it be?" said Kever. "Should we start with snakes or rides?"

I knew that I was trapped. If I were going to squeeze any pleasure at all from the evening, I knew I would have to discharge my part of the bargain first.

"Rides."

We headed away from the snake pit and down the midway.

I figured that I stood the best chance of surviving death by staying as close to the ground as possible. So each time Kever gestured towards a ride involving rockets that rose and spun around three or four storeys above the ground, I would shake my head and say, "Uh uh. Not *real* enough." Or, "No *imagination* to that one." This process of elimination allowed me to see virtually all of the rides in action before I chose.

There was one ride that seemed, at least in the noisy distance, gentle enough. As we approached it, the mechanism was slowing down, and I noticed right away that about half the riders were kids. So if a kid could take it, surely . . .

"What about that one?" I said.

"El Tarantula?"

"Yeah."

El Tarantula seemed to be built for low-altitude cruising. Like its namesake, it had eight legs. These were about thirty feet long. A double seat was rivetted to the end of each leg. So Kever and I could sit together in case I needed some fast anxiety-management therapy.

"Are you sure?" she said.

"What do you mean, am I sure?"

"Okay," said Kever. "The Tarantula it is."

We lined up at a booth and got tickets.

"What did you mean, 'Are you sure'?"

"Nothing," said Kever. "Here's your ticket."

"I mean, this ride, it won't . . ."

"No. Really. It's okay. It's just that . . ."

A surly fellow chewing on a cigar lifted a metal gate and showed us to our enclosure. He secured our seat by lowering a thick metal arm. It clanked like a door in a Hollywood cell block.

Kever turned to me. She put her hand on my arm and said, "Now. The thing is, is: this ride can get a little. You know. Hairy. And—"

"Hairy?"

"You know."

"What?"

"It gets a little hairy."

"Hairy."

"Now, there's no use panicking."

"I'm not panicking."

"I know. Just stop. Listen."

"I'm not panicking!"

"I know you're not panicking! Now listen!"

We began to attract some attention from the kids nearby.

"Some people fight this thing every inch of the way," Kever explained. "Don't fight it. Don't get all clenched up and grip the safety bar like that. Just unclench yourself."

"I'm not all clenched up."

"My God. I give up."

"Okay, maybe I *am* clenched. Sort of. But what if I get flung into the air or something."

"They want you to feel that way on the Tarantula."

It started to get to me. The fact that she knew El Tarantula so well. As though it were a rite of passage for stunt men or something. El Tarantula began to move slowly around, and in response to this motion our seat began to turn. I comforted myself with the thought that our seat's motion was like the moon's rotation in response to the Earth's revolutions.

"So what do I do?" I said to Kever.

"Just go with it."

"Go with it."

Kever's words sounded like the advice a woman would give to a man on just about any topic, even the one you're probably thinking about right now. It also sounded, for some obscure reason, like a dialogue between an American and a Canadian.

"Yes. Just . . . let yourself go."

The ride began to revolve faster. I tried fiercely to go with it. The problem with letting myself go, I soon learned, was the resultant fear that I would somehow *lose* myself. It was un-Canadian to lose oneself. I would either get caught napping and get flung out into space, or I would be too *lost* to duck when a metal beam came flying my way, or . . .

"See what I mean?" said Kever with a smile.

"Yeah."

"Wheee!" she cried.

"Whee," I said.

I became aware that there was a voice with this contraption, a very loud one. The voice of El Tarantula was raving at us through his P.A. system in the glass booth adjacent to the monster machine. As far as I can remember, he was giving a demonic version of the same advice Kever offered to me.

Awright now, just dip into the electricity of the moment now, dip into the powa now, because this baby has the powa to send you into the ionosphere, it's the straight truth, El Tarantula take me home baby take me home, let's boogy let's tear let's have one hellacious bad time, Lo-ward have mercy!

The voice flung its crazed message out into the carnival for all to hear. In fact I had been hearing this same voice all night long, and until now I'd been able to shut it out. No more. It had become reality.

You kids havin fun? it growled.

"Yes!" cried some young voices.

Ywanna go fast?

"Yes!" cried some brats behind us.

"No!" I cried, and I meant it.

Kever laughed. She probably thought I was joking.

El Tarantula lurched into a higher gear, and in response our double seat began to spin out into the fairground and then back into the guts of the dreaded machine. All this to the growls of the crazed man in the booth. He growled like Wolfman Jack, but he wasn't spinning discs late into the summer night. He had his hands on the controls, and he was in control of us.

Oh, baby, you're gonna feel so bad, feel so bad, El Tarantula can make you feel good about feelin bad.

He was omnipotent. It was that simple.

Ywanna go fasta?

"Yes!" cried the teenagers in front of us.

"Yes!" cried Kever.

And then several ideas struck me all at once. The God thing. The great American revelation of horror. The mechanism that drove our very fates. *El Tarantula.* We were mere satellites as fragile as balsa wood planes flying at breakneck speed through a dark universe with asteroids drifting blindly by, and who was running the show? Who was at the centre of our solar system? Not the warming sun, not the Canadian prime minister with all his well-meaning assertions, not a caring God, but this growling degenerate in the glass booth with the megaphone clutched in his greasy paw.

Ya had enough?

"Nooooo!"

Ya think this doom machine'll go any fasta?

"Yes!"

Well, my friends, let's see what she can do! You people prepare ta meetcha doom! Oh Lo-ward, have mercy!

We accelerated into a dervish that sent our little seat into such a backspin that I could only clutch the safety bar and groan until the experience was over. But it simply would not end. The great machine roared and screamed like a dying malamute bitch, hurling us out and then yanking us back in and then again sending us out into the fairground with all the blind fancy of centrifugal force, and each time I was flung out and dragged back, something recently ingested came sluicing along for the ride just a minisecond later, as though my stomach and its contents were trying to catch up with the rest of my body. We went around and around for a long, long time.

Five minutes, as it turned out.

When the surly fellow with the well-chewed cigar butt came over to release us, I was aware of several things. I was alive, of course. I was unhurt. I had not vomited. I was drenched in sweat. And for some reason, my limbs had forgotten how to get up and walk. I tried to stand by moving back and forth on my seat like a very old man in a wheelchair or a tiny boy in a stroller.

Kever extended her hand. She looked a bit concerned.

"Are you okay?"

"I'm fine."

"Are you sure?"

"I'm sure."

"Because if you're not feeling well, we can go home."

"I'm fine. I just need to get walking again."

I was in fact not very fine at all, but I was damned if I'd let

Kever escape the snake house and the huge python on the midway. Fair was fair.

"We can go and find Will and go right home," said Kever with a sorrowful note in her voice.

"I'm okay!" I cried.

Drenched in sweat and still shaking, I nevertheless managed to stand and wobble down the midway with Kever. As we approached the snake pit and the short fellow with the python, I began to forget the dark revelation that had come to me in the clutches of El Tarantula. I was back on dry land. We walked up to the python man.

"Wanna hold my snake?" he said to Kever.

"Let him go first," she said, indicating me. Kever began to ready her camera.

I moved over to the short fellow, and he began to instruct me in the holding of a large python.

"Here," he said, "lemme put this big coil over your neck, see? Now lemme put Bobby's neck in your hand, see? Now we can wrap this other big coil around here like this, see? Good. Smile for d'camera."

Bobby was surprisingly heavy. He lay there placidly, draped around my shoulders, his forked tongue flicking out at the crowds from time to time. I began to feel rather courageous.

"Isn't he slimy?" said Kever.

"No. Feel him right there," I said.

This was the first conversation I'd ever had with Kever in which either one of us was holding a large python. A bit tentatively, Kever reached over and touched Bobby's neck. He extended his head in Kever's direction. The tongue went out and she brought her hand back. But without any urging from me, she reached forward again and stroked Bobby where his coils were thickest, almost as though Bobby were Pecos, her Malaysian cat.

"Your turn," I said to Kever.

The short fellow uncoiled Bobby from around my chest and shoulders and took him back into his own arms.

Kever approached me, keeping me between herself and Bobby.

She whispered in my ear, "You have to promise not to leave me. You have to stay right close, and if that snake shows any sign of aggression, you have to promise to take it off me. Promise?"

"Of course," I said, all masculine courage and gentleness. "Just remember," I said, paraphrasing my brother, "snakes may be cold-blooded but they take on the temperature of whatever they're touching. They like the feel of a warm body. Just holding a snake establishes a sort of kinship."

Ah, the wisdom I was spouting! The authority! I almost wanted to take notes.

Slowly our little man with the drooping moustache and I helped Kever on with her new friend Bobby. Kever kept her cool. When the last coil was in place and Bobby was comfortably draped over Kever's shoulders, she whispered, "Remember, stay close."

I stood close and watched with pride as Kever stared in wonder at Bobby's flicking tongue. After a moment, I backed away just far enough to snap a picture. Snake Woman, I would call it.

I still have the picture. In it Kever is both cringing and smiling. She can not *believe* that this is happening.

It was still rather hot, and I was wondering how best to cool off when along came Will. He'd been sampling some of the rides, but there was one ride he was saving for me—if I would care to join him.

"The single ferris wheel," he said, pointing towards the sunset. "It's a good place to cool off."

The single (as opposed to the double) ferris wheel was, of course, too tame for Kever.

"Do you think you'd like to go up on the ferris wheel with me, Dave?"

As I've mentioned, Will is autistic. He is six foot five or more, and he has a guileless manner that makes it hard to say no to anything. So I forgot about my apocalyptic experience in El Tarantula and agreed to go up with Will. I knew I could once again get a case of the clenches, and I didn't want to stretch my luck in yet another infernal machine, but I got on board with Will. We could be astronauts together.

Up we went, up above the neon midway, and gazed at the sunset and gawked around at the spangled city to the north of us. There was a gentle breeze coming off the prairie and a skinny fingernail moon rising in the east. The breeze was fragrant with hay and clover. It washed over my face and began to cool my body. I was not afraid.

Will was waving. I looked down and saw Kever waving up to us. She seemed rather pleased that her son and her boyfriend were being astronauts together. She was probably pleased that she had come through the snake pit ordeal so bravely. Snakes and tarantulas. We had met them head-on and contended just fine.

"Over there," said Will. "That's Sion. I went there for two years."

He was pointing to the northeast. I couldn't make out the school, but I pretended that I could. Sion, another name for Zion.

"There were some pretty wild kids there," said Will.

"Did they ever bother you?"

"Once a bunch of them beat me up."

"Boy, Will, that must have been scary for you. Did you have to go right back the next day?"

"I went back the next day, but Mom didn't *make* me go back. I just made up my mind."

"Did you like that school?"

"Sometimes."

We began our final descent and I could no longer look for the place where Sion stood. Wasn't Sion a centre of Jewish enlightenment? King David's metaphor for heaven? Perhaps, but maybe not for the faint of heart. I got out of the seat and followed Will up to where his mum stood. She gave him a proud-mum hug. There they were. My two Americans.

"How'd you like that one?" said Kever. "Slow enough for you?"

I strove for a lordly tone. "It was fine. A good spot for philosopher-kings to view their kingdom."

"It was great," said Will. "David wasn't even scared."

A Piece of Quartz Crystal

SATURDAY, AUGUST 3. Grey rags drift across the prairie, nebulous and dull as dryer lint. Not clouds today but *nuages*. Draw out the word for several yawny seconds. Perfect day for reading instruction manuals.

SUNDAY, AUGUST 4. Light rain. A sky of leaden gloom. Ideal conditions for brooding over the death of summer.

MONDAY, AUGUST 5. Great grey layers of slutswool ranged all the way down the horizon. The clouds have the precise shape and woolly texture of dreams from a sheep's brain. On such days the sheep fall asleep counting clouds.

TUESDAY, AUGUST 6. Unstable weather, changeable clouds. Name them like pet seals as they churn past our little atoll. Stratocumulus. Stratonimbus. Altocumulus. Cirronimbus. Today is Everybody's Weather. It's cloudseal oceans   I recall   I really don't know clouds' atoll.

WEDNESDAY, AUGUST 7. Dreamt last night of Lake Louise. That eighteen-year-old feeling. No clouds today. Deep sky blue from stem to gudgeon. A clean slate, you might say. Perfect day to begin something.

Let me begin. I am at St. Peter's Abbey. No negotiations at the gate. You just knock and then a-walk on in. The presiding spirit of this version of paradise is Father Peter. A few years ago he was running the Prairie Messenger and fiddling with computers. But wasn't he the guestmaster then? And wasn't he the captain of the abbey's baseball team? And didn't we see him on a tractor, heading for a field of potatoes?

Now he is the Abbott. Peterabott, they like to say. Yesterday he was either in Brazil or just returned from Brazil. Perhaps both. There is no general agreement. Peter is like Chicken Man. *He's everywhere, he's everywhere!* Everywhere smiling in his black soutane, everywhere fierce in his badminton shorts. Everywhere like his Boss, the Cloudsmith.

At this precise moment, Peter is at vespers. This is hard fax, as they say in the news business. I know, because I am there too, singing and taking notes in my pew.

The holy men chant beneath the arched ceiling of a high chapel, which hums beneath the great blue vault of the sky. Priests and monks in black robes. Most of them are over fifty, many over seventy, a handful over ninety. Their voices are faint, strong, discordant, rich, on key, off key, everyone's voice a few minutes out of sleep and echoing like voices in the catacombs.

This cathedral and this abbey are one mile east and south of the town of Muenster, Saskatchewan. The prairie all around Muenster is grain and willows from horizon to horizon—all except for the vast canola fields of squinting yellow. And of course our little atoll, St. Peter's. It is run by Benedictines, who are famous throughout the world for their hospitality.

The abbey is the size of a large farm. It has forests with mazes, big meadows with wildflowers and apiaries for the annual honey harvest. It has a ravine and a pond in the woods next to the railroad tracks and a series of pig barns and corrals for horses, pens for chickens, a patchwork of fields for vegetables and a sizable orchard for berries and apples and plums—all this grown and processed by the brothers and fathers. They even make their own wine from the fruit in their orchard.

There's a baseball diamond and a track for runners and an academic college and a cathedral in the middle of the property.

Where, right now, the Benedictine brethren are still at their vespers, and so am I, this evening's token sinner.

I don't smirk about my status as a non-Catholic. An agnostic, actually. I don't feel as though I'm a secret agent for nonbelievers. I'm always humbled by the openness of these Benedictines, who play host to so many artists and writers, year after year. They don't just tolerate us; they spend time with us. Willingly, I suspect. They don't catechize, but their doors are always open.

If you want to pass the time watching clouds, you need only wander along one of the mazes out to where the trees stop and stand at the edge of the prairie. Or you can climb up to the bell tower and gaze out at the copper light of August. You can't do this in Saskatoon unless you live in a high-rise. And in a high-rise you can't smell the wind coming off the grass bringing in the scent of aspen rot, the residue of last week's mown hay, the musky perfume of the sloughs.

Coming here is my August ritual. All through the year, though August is the best time, artists and writers come here to finish work and to recharge their batteries. They are lodged in what used to be the convent, a small brick residence surrounded by high car-raganas. It has ten monastically spare rooms and a small chapel with a pump organ. This chapel has now become a library. Each writer is given a room, to live and work in. In addition to their rooms, the artists are given studios on the top floor of the college. The meals are cheap and wholesome and the clouds are free.

When you arrive at the convent, you haul your stuff into your room, hoping for one that's shaded from the ripening August sun. The room will be a plain little space with a crucifix on the wall and perhaps a religious motto or two. The walls will be painted in absolutely the wrong colours—pick your worst. The little bed will have a grass-green polyester coverlet. You strip off the coverlet, wrap it up and place it in your closet.

The process of unpacking in a holy place is under way. It's a delicious process, so you don't mind dragging it out. You *want* to drag it out. Unpack your clothes. These are very casual. A sweater for hailstorms and their chilly aftermath. Shorts for hot weather, badminton and volleyball. Sweatpants and jeans and T-shirts, all the ragged clothes that proclaim to your fellow writers and artists that you are a real casual guy and not the slightest bit bourgeois. Lift out the books, stack them in the bookcase. Place the laptop on the big table, printer right next to it on the small table. Connect them both.

Oh, you are going to be inspired in this place.

That crucifix. Is it going to make you feel sinful or something? Shouldn't you place it in one of your drawers? Bring it out for inspiration when nothing else works? No?

Leave it there.

Your manuscript, the big one, the one that glows in the dark, the one that will put you over the top this time. Put it next to your books on the shelf where (the room is so small!) you can reach it without having to leave your chair. Your wooden plain straight-backed chair. Seat of wisdom for the next three weeks. Place this manuscript, for good luck, between Munro and Shields.

The pens and Scotch tape and erasers and push pins and paper clips and your Donald Duck stapler and your elastics and bottle of white-out, all the things you find in a writer's desk drawer: put them in the drawer that comes with your table.

Your special totem. Hm.

(Pause for contemplation.)

This is the lucky object with which this year's manuscript seems to be bonding. You know: the little soapstone loon, the freeze-dried scorpion, the rubber shrunken head from your adolescence, the rusty wobbler you flung into the cattails to catch your biggest pike, the hair jewellery from your weird sweet aunt. You place this object on top of your glowing manuscript that lies between Munro and Shields and you pray that it will bring luck all through the night as you dream. A pagan prayer, of course. About as Christian and selfless as the prayer uttered by a boxer who wants to dismantle the fellow in the opposing corner, who is also praying.

This year's totem is a piece of quartz crystal from a mountain cave somewhere west of Lake Louise.

Hm.

Warren Cariou carries himself taut and humming like a bowstring. Right now he's shifting furniture in the next room. He wants to beat Father Peter in badminton. So do I. He wants to complete work on a novella. So do I. He knows that this time he'll connect with his Muse in a way that he's never connected before.

So do I.

My novella. This is a story I've been working and reworking since 1988. In fact, it has elements of a story I wrote in 1965, finished in a dishevelled first draft and never sent off. Thank God. Each version of this story calls on my memories dating back to 1960 and 1961, when I was a carhop and a cab driver in the mountains. I've forgotten most of what really happened back then, but I retain a vivid impression of who I was and an equally strong impression of a parallel existence. *A young man I could have been.*

He grew up in Edmonton. He played a ukulele. He did impressions of James Stewart, Arthur Godfrey and Premier Ernest C. Manning. He had no politics at all, which made him fair game in various quests for the possession of his soul. Ardent socialists and zealous capitalists claimed him for their own. As always, he listened. *The less government the better.* Yeah, why not? *Universal medicare.* Now there's a neat idea.

Almost no one noticed or remembered him from these years. He was a terminal romantic, but not a good bet for romantic lead. He was built for yearning and not for love. A head full of romantic dreams and a body full of hormones, sustained by beer and cheeseburgers. This year's chronic innocent. A listener, a brooder, a follower. He had a tendency to go moralistic on all questions that required a gift for complexity or a measure of worldliness.

I (he, we) arrived at the Chateau Lake Louise in early May of 1960. A sodden, snowy day. For the first time in my life, I gazed up at the Victoria Glacier. A great grey amphitheatre as big as a galaxy, booming with avalanches and obscured by clouds. I must have experienced some prairie-boy wonder at that scene. The highest reaches of the chateau merging with the gloom of low-lying clouds—and it just disappeared! All day I kept off the chill with mugs of coffee, breathed in the larchy air and became a great openmouthed yearning happy fool. Mountain madness.

My nickname at that time was Scale, a derivative of Scaley Carp. I bore this name patiently because I was so insecure that *any* nickname was welcome.

It happened like this. Mike McNulty and I were having a gab outside the main door of the Chateau Lake Louise. I admired McNulty because he owned a small green sports car called a Sprite and because he was a cynic. He tolerated me because I was deferential to a fault and because he thought I was funny. It was early August, probably around midnight. We were tired. It was the end of a late shift, and McNulty was waiting for a man whose car he had brought up from the parking lot.

McNulty said to me, "Are you going down to the roast?"

"Where?"

"Great Divide Campground. It'll go on way past midnight."

"Nah," I said. "I'm bagged. You going down there?"

"Guess not. Kinda late."

Then McNulty added, "The Lake O'Hara girls will be there."

I shrugged. I had no idea who the Lake O'Hara girls were.

At last the man came down for his car. He was tall, well built, about fifty. He had a florid face and wavy silver hair. He wore a white dinner jacket and he was a little tight from his revels in the hotel. He looked at us.

What he saw was a pair of carhops. We both wore blue serge pants and jackets with the Grayline crest on the breast pocket. We both had brush cuts shaved very close. McNulty was a small dapper fellow—so dapper, in fact, that even in his Grayline blues he looked like a Harvard blueblood. I was a taller, gormless version of McNulty. Perhaps we were both gawking at this distinguished fellow, this playboy.

He was obviously a playboy, the real McCoy. For one thing, he looked like he could *afford* to be a playboy. And although he smelled a bit like a distillery, we were not really put off by the man. Perhaps we should have been, but he was what some of my friends referred to as a neat guy.

The man fixed us both with his glazed eyes and said something like the following: "What I wouldn't give to be as young as you fellas. Up here with all these girls. Take my advice. For God's sake, have all the fun you can when you're still young enough to enjoy it."

The man had spoken with such sadness, such embarrassing candour, that I had to wonder if he weren't an American. But American or not, his words hit home. Even McNulty, who was an intellectual snob and scoffed at everything as a rule, went silent when the man drove off. This neat guy in the white dinner jacket was the approximate age of our parents, and in one short speech he had told me everything my parents had feared I might learn away from home. In my shallow repressed undergraduate heart, I must have harboured a secret desire. It was contained in this man's hedonistic message. He smelled of gin, he was a self-indulgent playboy, he looked like he was born to cause divorce and heartache—he had these sad occasions written all over his face— but he was *carpe diem* in the flesh.

This is an August memory. It has a peculiarly August poignancy to it. The summer is dying, the nights are getting cool. Youth is dying. There's a late night roast at the Great Divide Campground. The Lake O'Hara girls have come down for it. The Lake O'Hara girls.

You guessed it. McNulty and I were gone in a flash, down to the Great Divide.

Well past midnight, I found myself sitting by the campfire between Judy Waitress and Judy Chambermaid. They were both from Nanaimo, B.C., and this was their first time down from the lodge at Lake O'Hara to Lake Louise.

"Where, exactly, is Lake O'Hara?" I said to to Judy Waitress.

"Hold it still," she said.

She was pouring beer, meant for me, into a very large milk-shake container until it was two-thirds full. Then she made me hold the container steady so that she could turn my beer into a porch-climber by adding about a glassful of Jordan's Branvin port, which sold back then for ninety-five cents a bottle.

Judy Waitress was, of course, a waitress. She had freckles and long brown hair that was very curly and beautiful and out of control—chaotic hair that she complained about and tossed over her shoulders as though someone with no brains at all had imposed it on her. She was almost unbearably cute.

"Lake O'Hara? It's this beautiful lake up over there." She pointed to a star that twinkled somewhere above the Great Divide.

"There's two ways of getting to Lake O'Hara. You can walk from the front of the Chateau Lake Louise all the way to the top of the Victoria Glacier, elevation eleven thousand feet, and basically ski downhill until you crash into our lodge."

"Which Mr. Ford frowns on," said Judy Chambermaid.

"Which Mr. Ford frowns on. Or . . . you can pay five dollars and take the alpine bus up the road."

"Which Mr. Ford *doesn't* frown on," said Judy Chambermaid.

"Which Mr. Ford doesn't frown on," said Judy Waitress.

The second Judy (Chambermaid) was, of course, a chambermaid, and she wore a heavy wool sweater with a snowflake design. She had short sensible hair, which was also beautiful. We three settled into our porch-climbers so nicely that all the world became a wiener roast and we the only people that mattered. The Lake O'Hara girls had become beautiful before my very eyes. Their presence took the chill out of the night.

Why were the older, more experienced guys not buzzing around these girls? Why hadn't they cut them out of the herd before I arrived? Why was I allowed to come so close to such perfection? I don't remember. If beauty is indeed in the eye of the beholder, well, perhaps I was the only beholder. Or perhaps, as often happened up there, the supply of girls exceeded the demand.

Or perhaps the Lake O'Hara girls, having checked out the other Grayline drivers and having found them to be a pretty randy crew, well, perhaps they found me to be a pretty safe bet. Nonthreatening. Perhaps even "cute," under the right circumstances (night vision, porch-climbers).

Along came the driver of their alpine bus and mentioned to the Judies that he was heading back up to Lake O'Hara.

"Are you Mr. Ford?" I said to the fellow.

"No," said Judy Chambermaid, rising from her picnic bench. "This guy is Bob Big Bus."

I shook hands with Bob Big Bus, who seemed like a nice fellow. At this stage of the proceedings (one porch-climber too many) almost everyone at the campground seemed a nice fellow or gal. But I was missing the point. Bob Big Bus was telling the Judies that this was their last chance to ride home with him. That is why Judy Chambermaid was now standing and gathering her things together. She smiled tenderly and knowingly.

"We have to go," she said.

"Now?" cried Judy Waitress. (My, but her freckles were fetching!)

"Now," sighed Judy Chambermaid.

"We just got here," cried Judy Waitress.

"You've been saying that for the last two hours," sighed Judy Chambermaid.

"C'mon," said Bob Big Bus. "Rally."

"I'm too tired to rally," said Judy Waitress. "The might is but a nolecule."

She rose to her feet and gave me a little hug. "Well, Scale, it was real."

Until this moment my nickname had been a thing to be endured. But coming as it did from the lips of Judy Waitress, this name seemed suddenly a term of sweetest endearment. She tossed back her great wonderful mane of hair and made as if to follow the other two back to the alpine bus.

"You can't go now," I said to her.

"I have to."

"Why?"

"I told you."

I must have seemed a bit of a slow learner to Judy Waitress. She told me again. About the alpine bus being the only vehicle allowed up the road etcetera. But I was hearing a man in a white dinner jacket saying something about gathering rosebuds while ye may.

Apparently I made a speech. I have witnesses. The speech was delivered to Judy Waitress but was loud enough for the equally impaired lot around the campfire to hear. My speech was impelled by Eros and porch-climbers, and to anyone with even a touch of rhetorical subtlety, my words could likely have been consigned to the cliché bucket. But porch-climbers do not, as a rule, tend to sharpen the critical faculties, and my small audience found no fault with my entreaty to Judy Waitress. I spoke to her of such things as the fleeting of summer, the brevity of youth and beauty (the grave's a fine and private etcetera), the fact that if she went back to Lake O'Hara I might never get to know her more intimately—

"Know me more intimately?" she said.

"I don't even know your real last name."

"Oh."

I spoke of memories in old age. I constructed a hypothetical scene, A.D. 2020, when she was in her twilight years, speaking to her grandchildren, recounting to their young ears this very crossroads in our lives. And would she say to little Annie and sweet Deirdre *NO*, we did *not* stay behind at the Great Divide campground to get to know each other? We went instead back to separate cold bunks divided from each other by a huge eleven-thousand-foot glacier? No? We only *wished* we had stayed together at the roast? Or would she say to this wide-eyed gathering of burgeoning youth . . . (dramatic pause) *Yes.* Yes, to keeping the party going. Yes, to getting to know each other. Yes, we said yes to life itself.

I remember some applause at this point in my speech. It would be so like me to insert this moment of glory into my account and later call it memory. But. Applause, yes. I remember applause of the porch-climber *carpe diem* variety.

"You don't understand," said Judy.

By that time she was the only Judy left at the campground because Bob Big Bus had given up on her and driven off into the night with Judy Chambermaid and the other Lake O'Hara girls. I must have realized that I would have to do something responsible to set Judy's mind at rest.

"I've got an idea," I said.

She looked at me with the sort of exasperation one feels in the presence of the irrepressible. *You don't understand.*

"No, seriously," I cried. "I have the answer. McNulty!"

"McNulty?"

"Yes."

What Judy didn't know was that McNulty had his green Sprite here at the campground. If any car could drive up the steep road to Lake O'Hara, the green Sprite could do it.

"McNulty!" I cried out in every general direction. "McNulty!"

"Maybe he's gone home," said Judy.

"He can't be gone. His car is still here."

"I don't see what—"

"McNulty! *McNulty!*"

I roamed up and down among the rows of necking couples sprawled around by the fire, some of them rolled up in blankets and thrashing in sleeping bags.

"Have you seen McNulty?"

"Bugger off."

"Have you seen McNulty?"

"He drowned in the Bow River."

"Have you seen McNulty?"

"#%**!"

"Have you seen McNulty?"

"Piss up a rope."

After interrupting enough rutting youth to retard the illegitimate birth rate for the entire valley, I just gave up and sat with

Judy by the fire. I know we did some cautious kissing. She always
closed her eyes first. It was almost too delightful to bear. And then,
from a blanket near our feet, there came a voice. Female, exasperated. "Are you the guy lookin for McNulty?"

"Well, yeah—"

"Don't touch this blanket!" cried the same voice.

Judy pulled me back before I had revealed anything too scan-
dalous beneath the blanket.

"What is it exactly that you want from McNulty?" said the
voice.

"I want the keys to his car," I said. "Emersion of missy."

"Emersion of Missy?"

"A mission of mercy, you retard," said Judy.

She got a bad case of the giggles and we both lost it for a
minute. A long, bare arm emerged like a moray from the folds of
the blanket, jingling a set of keys before my eyes. I took the keys.

"Thank you," I said.

"You're welcome," the voice replied.

"You see?" I said to Judy. "You see? Hey?"

She bent over as though to look at her shoes and shook her
head *no no no* until her entire head was obscured by her hair.

When she came up for air, she was still smiling. "You don't
understand, Scale."

And then she gave up trying to explain anything to me and we
went off into the bush and necked and partied and fell in love and
sent a large animal crashing through the underbrush and got lost.
Then we found our way back from the bush and continued to
party with the last of the partiers and did a long chorus for
McNulty, who was still missing in action:

> *we know what you're doing*
> *we know what you're doing*

All things considered, a pretty good night.

When Judy and I piled into McNulty's Sprite we were both

perilously close to sober. It was pretty cold. I wheeled the little green car off from the campground and away from the Great Divide. In the space of fifty feet we had crossed over from Alberta to British Columbia. To Albertans with notions of high living and elegant lifestyles, British Columbia was the Promised Land. Maybe to the expectant capitalists of the world Alberta meant oil revenues and fast bucks, but to us it also meant hard work and harder winters. British Columbia meant leisure. Lotusland. Luxury.

Driving west with Judy next to me in the Sprite, I had a vision of moving out to Vancouver Island and settling forever in the bosom of Lotusland and in close proximity to the bosoms of my new love. I saw my entire future as though the mayor of Nanaimo had handed me the key to the city. I turned to Judy and realized that I was too sober to say what I had to say.

"Scale, are you feeling okay?" she said.

"This is the happiest we'll ever be for the rest of our lives."

"Just watch your driving. The turnoff's about a mile up the road."

I said it again, a sad three A.M. drunk. "This is the happiest time of our lives. We have to live. Live!"

"Isn't that what Gooch said in *Auntie Mame?*" said Judy. " 'Live'?"

"Live!"

"Live!"

"Live!"

"Turn there!"

I wheeled the little Sprite up a gravel road.

"Slow down! There's a gate!"

I hit the brakes and ground to a gravelly stop just a foot or two from a bright silver obstruction.

"What the hell is this thing doin here?"

"I told you!" said Judy.

"Yeah, but how do we get up to Lake O'Hara?"

"Remember what I said? You either have to walk in or ride with Bob Big Bus."

"Oh."

"And now I have to walk up the trail in the dark. If I don't, I'll miss my morning shift in the dining room. Jeez."

"I'll walk you home. No sweat."

"No."

"Yes. I mean it. You always walk your date up to the door, right? Even in Alberta."

"No. You shouldn't. It's okay."

"I *mean* it. *I'm going to walk you home and that's all there is to it.*" It was great sounding like such a take charge sort of guy.

"I mean, what if you ran into a bear or something? Seriously. I am going to walk you home."

"Well, Scale, that's real nice of you."

"Aw."

We got out of the car, and Judy went off into the bush. I thought she was just going for a pee, but when she came back she was holding a couple of large sticks she had broken off from a dead tree.

"You might need one of these," she said.

"What for?"

"As a hiking stick. It's mostly kind of um . . . uphill?"

There was something vaguely apologetic in her tone.

We began to walk up the trail.

"Ah, Judy?"

"Yes?"

"How far is this?"

She looked straight ahead and said, "About eight miles."

"Eight miles? One way?"

"I told you."

Eight miles in the dark along a gravel road, mostly uphill, at three in the morning is certainly one way to get to know a person more intimately. Trudging up the steepest hills we had little breath for conversation, but each time the road levelled off a bit, we found out all kinds of things about each other. I only wish I could remember them, because whatever we said to each other seemed quite important at the time.

I remember what we didn't talk about: we declared a moratorium, for as long as it remained dark, on any bear conversations.

We rose higher and higher along the road towards the very top of the treeline, and by four or five in the morning we could see our breath. At last a trace of light began to rise back in the direction of the Alberta Rockies. We stopped to drink from a waterfall on O'Hara Creek. We were somewhere beyond weariness, but when at last we rounded the corner between the warden's cabin and Lake O'Hara Lodge, we both cheered.

Just as the sun was rising I found myself leaning against the door frame of the O'Hara staff cabin, smiling into the face of Judy Waitress. I wonder if morning hadn't begun to undo the night's mischievous work. We did exchange addresses, I remember that. And she gave me a piece of quartz crystal she had found in a nearby cave as a keepsake.

In a few minutes I would be going back down the hill, eight miles, to McNulty's Sprite. Perhaps I just smiled at her and she at me. Adventurer to adventurer. And then she made her excuses and said that she had to change into her waitressing uniform, so we said goodbye.

I needed a rest, and so I found a bench overlooking the lake and just for a moment closed my eyes. I breathed in. A breeze greeted my nostrils. It had come all the way down from the glacial heights of Wiwaxy or Cathedral Mountain and descended like the breath of God to the alpine meadows, picking up the exhalations of each moist organism in all the gurgling alpine places; it had breathed through the forests of larch, tamarack, juniper and pine. The fragrance was more delightful than any I had ever given myself over to. It smelled green.

I opened my eyes. Down by the shore the lake was green. A green as green as Scarlet O'Hara's eyes, green as all Ireland. A pale greyish-green around the edges and in the shoals, a ponderous green in the middle. The breeze descended on the water, a cloud passed over the rising sun, and suddenly the water was turquoise.

The cloud passed, the sun returned, and the water was several shades of green.

Judy was my first love. This lake granted me my first glance at perfect beauty. She and the lake are forever intertwined, a part of my green remembering.

I realized then that I might never see her again. She would go back to Nanaimo to attend Malaspina College or UVic and live among the coastal mists and exotic vistas of Lotusland. I would return to the Prairies. I wasn't a man with plans of his own; I was still somebody's son.

Perhaps I walked all the way back to McNulty's Sprite with this in mind. All the way back to my side of the Great Divide. Waking up, like Bottom, to the memory of a perfect dream. Whatever else I thought about, one thing was clear: my future lay on the grey side of the Great Divide.

When people move to Saskatchewan from somewhere else they sometimes acquire a lost look. I know that look. I wore it from the moment I moved into my apartment in City Park in the summer of 1975.

"Do you miss Alberta?" people would say.

"I miss the mountains," I would say, remembering *my* mountains at Lake Louise. I miss Lake O'Hara. I miss my dream of moving to Lotusland, the one I never allowed to happen. I miss 1960. It was a very good year. I miss Paradise.

Nothing is quite so boring as people who wish they were back home where the real action is. Nothing is quite so sad as people who wish they were somewhere else. And so you move on, and lo, one night lying on a hillside in the Qu'Appelle Valley you and your beloved are gazing up at a meteor shower. You have the intimacy you had so often yearned for, and you are reminded of something that happened thirty-five years ago in the mountains . . .

An eighteen-year-old boy at the wheel of a green Sprite turns to a tired girl with freckles and says *this is the happiest we'll ever be for the rest of our lives.*

You wonder why, if he is so damned happy, his tone is so sad. And you realize, of course, that he was wrong. You have probably known this for some time, but tonight beneath the throbbing prairie cosmos, you are sure. Anyone with any brains at all would know without thinking that Paradise is right here. On this hillside. Beside this gal.

Or, believe it or not, in this monastery. Gazing at this manuscript. Held down by this piece of quartz crystal. Today. August 8, 1995.

PART FOUR

Fall

CARPE DIEMS

FIRST, A CONFESSION. I am one of the nasally challenged. I grew up with a twisted cartilage in my nose. I must have taken one right hook too many in my roughhousing youth. My septal cartilage takes a dramatic turn to the right, constricting the air supply so that my right nostril is always getting blocked. These blockages have led to a plague of sinus infections and head colds and a lack of sleep in recent years. In 1995, at the end of August, I had an operation, a pretty common procedure, I'm told. The surgeon snipped off some polyps way up in my nostrils, cut away some cartilage, widened both nostrils and corrected the constriction in my nose.

I remember the last minute or two before going under. My surgeon, Peter Spafford, and his small crew were gathered around my head in a relaxed and familiar conversation. They sounded entirely comfortable with one another and with this procedure. They seemed to have a routine down. I felt almost cocky with confidence. Just before the last bit of Pentathol slipped into my veins, I was going to grin up at them and say, *Let's get in there and kick some butt.*

"Peter tells me you're a trout fisherman," said one of the nurses.

"Yes," I said. "In about two weeks I'm heading up to Narrow Hills for my fall fishing trip."

"In a few seconds your vision will go a bit wonky," Peter warned.

Indeed, just as he spoke, the lights above my head began to separate and multiply like the start of a movie flashback.

"If I were to go up there and fish for pickerel, where would I go?" said the nurse.

I knew the answer to that one. It was a lovely round lake surounded by gentle hills and an immense forest. You take a bumpy winding road off the main highway; it's about a half a mile and all downhill. It has a Cree name, and the name was just under the surface of the lake's tiny ripples.

When I regained consciousness it was the afternoon and someone was speaking to me. I tried to say, "Lake Ispuchow." The name of the lake came out all wrong or hardly at all. My voice couldn't seem to escape my sinus cavities. It was trapped up there. Why should my voice be trapped up there?

I had a brief flash of a dream while I was under the knife. There was a stream and a September blue sky, some leafy bushes and a single, leafless willow branch rising vertically and bent like a flyrod. In the dream I gave a mighty clearing of my throat. A whole moment of savage throat clearing. Had I done that in my operation?

"Mr. Carpenter, how do you feel?"

It was a nurse, but not the one who had wanted to know where the pickerel were.

"O-hay," I said.

I was in a ward with three elderly men. We had all been in surgery that day, that was obvious. None of the men said very much, and when they tried to talk to their visitors they sounded pretty feeble. One of these old guys, who went by the name of Wally, had a catheter draining blood and urine into a large container.

It grew dark outside, Kever gave me a good night kiss, our visitors went home, and the lights went out. At this time our curtains were all pulled back, so with a little effort I could see my three roommates in their beds. This was possible because of the light from 20th Street, a feeble bluish glow from the stores and street lamps. The effect on our faces was so ghastly that I'm sure we all looked rather close to the grave. Of course, I had no way of knowing just how close to the grave my companions were, only that on that particular night they all looked and sounded like death warmed over.

My nostrils were packed so that I could only breathe through my mouth. This, and the fact that unchecked blood is a major irritant, made my throat very dry—so dry and raw, in fact, that I had to take a sip of water about every ten minutes. I remained either awake or dozing in short fits throughout the entire night.

The old fellow kitty-corner from my bed, the aforementioned Wally, was having a particularly rough night. He couldn't seem to get comfortable. When at last he fell asleep, he awoke groaning and muttering.

Through my packed nostrils I said, "Are you aw-wight?"

"Yep," he said carefully.

With his catheter tube leaking blood and urine, his pallid face and scruffy dishevelled hair, Wally looked about as healthy as a specimen in an anatomy lab. A little later he seemed to fall back into a troubled sleep. I might have dozed off between sips. I awoke to see him struggling to take his clothes off. He went about it very slowly and meticulously, so I didn't say anything. Wally had to navigate his way vertical with a catheter tube coming from a bandaged area on his abdomen and an IV tube sprouting from his arm. But he managed to do it, to stand up and make his way naked with slow penguin steps around the side of his bed. His pajamas hung from his IV tube like articles on a clothesline. Muttering all the way, he got around the side of his bed and growled a few words about getting the hell out of here. Suddenly, he was brought up short by the tug of his IV tube.

"Are you o-hay?" I said.

"Oh," said Wally. He had been sleepwalking.

"Shull I hall the lurse?" I said.

"Thank you, yes," he said dreamily, not like a man, but like a wakeful spirit. Indeed, he did not walk back to his bed; he *drifted* back.

I pushed my emergency button, the nurse came in, saw immediately that the naked man was sleepwalking, and bundled him back into bed.

Wally *drifted* back to sleep. The man in the next cot *drifted* to the bathroom and *drifted* back to bed. In the ghastly light from 20th Street, we were all drifting in and out of sleep like disembodied souls.

Several times during the night, because I was awake, I had to go over to my sleepwalking friend and lead him back to bed. Each time, in his sleep, Wally thanked me. Awake or asleep, Wally was always a gentleman.

When breakfast came we were all asleep, and we woke up to see each other in the more accustomed light of day. I was rather surprised to see that we were all going about breakfast as though we planned to live for a while. In fact, by about 9:00 A.M. there were little conversations going back and forth between the beds.

"Wook at us!" I proclaimed. "We lidn't die affer all!"

I got some knowing chuckles from my three roommates.

After a day and a half in hospital, my doctor sent me home. I had some real fast healing to do. My incentive was our annual September fishing trip up at Narrow Hills Park. Of all my reasons for being, this is numero uno. I am nothing if not a September troutster.

For two weeks I was an impatient patient. My doctor pronounced me fit, but because my energy level was still low, I was to take it easy.

Yeah. Sure.

September 14, 1995, arrived and I was packed and ready. Kever had to drive up to Creighton, a northern community near Flin Flon. As luck would have it, our friends' camp on Little Bear Lake and Kever's destination were both up on the Hanson Lake road. She was able to drive me right to the doorstep of Bob Calder's cabin. She would return there two days later after judging an art show and join us for some fishing. In the meantime, while I waited for the crew to start trickling in from Saskatoon, I would light the fire, prepare supper and gather fishing information. Even if my body was not responding with that characteristic flood of energy that I feel on every fishing trip, my mind was gathering its own kind of enthusiasm. I'd been off painkillers and anti-inflammatory drugs for a week. The only drug I'd had in several days was a single aspirin. My appetite was coming back.

I was coming back.

I lit the fire, unpacked the food and began to assemble the ingredients for a stew that night. I had enough stewing beef, but (having seen some grouse out by the highway) I began to think, what a great idea if I could bag a grouse for the stew!

I went for a short walk into the bush and the grouse were everywhere. Ruffed grouse and spruce grouse and a flock of sharptails. As heedless as the ancient mariner, I brought down a spruce grouse and carried it back to the yard. It was a lovely male with scarlet combs above the eyes. It was bleeding from the beak, and because the blood had just passed through the bird's lungs, it bubbled out an amazing bright red. I gutted and skinned the bird, boned it for the stew, and, with a certain woodsman's pride, awaited the arrival of my friends.

One was our host, Bob Calder. He was to arrive around the same time as Ken Bindle and Ken's daughter, Judith Wright. Ken used to raise and sell trout in his own private hatchery. Ken Bindle is my trout guru. His practical knowledge about the habits of trout is so extensive I have become his willing student.

Two others, who would arrive the next evening ahead of Kever, were Paul and Julie Bidwell. Paul, who has the smile (though not nearly the size) of the actor John Goodman, had recently been made chair of the English Department, and Calder and I thought that he needed a break from the mind-numbing challenges of chairmanship. His wife, Julie, is a nurse with a great love for northern canoeing and camping.

Judith, her son, Liam, Ken and Calder finally arrived, and by the time the bunch of us sat down to eat, it was dark out. They all admired my grouse stew, and I must have gone to bed with a self-satisfied smile on my face. It's not often we see so many grouse up here that we can just shoot one or bring one down with the nearest convenient missile. Yes, it had been a nice arrival.

The next day, Bob and Ken and I took Ken's boat up to Mitten Lake. We had heard about its legendary brook trout, and we wanted to try them out. The rumour was that they were uncatchable. I *love* lakes like that. This one is long and narrow, and the bottom drops off sharply in the middle. It's very clear, boggy water, and it reminds me of the lochs in northern Scotland. When we arrived, this little lake was as unrippled as a sheet of ice, but when we got out onto the lake in Ken's rowboat, the wind descended on us like the wrath of God. We fought this wind all through the middle of the day, and I started to get a chill.

What kept me out there, when I should have known better, was the fact that I had a reputation for endurance on cold fishing days and the fact that we had had several tentative nibbles. Finally, Bob Calder latched onto a large fish, and my shivers were forgotten. The fish ran deep and sulky. Bob had to fight for every inch of line, but gradually the brookie came up and we got the net under it. An amazing fish, almost eighteen inches long and weighing exactly three pounds. We had broken the jinx of Mitten Lake.

I began to show signs of waning, so we came in to shore and had some lunch. When this happens, you get out of the wind and move around as much as you can. The food and the activity will usually warm you up and you're ready to go again. At least this is the way *my* body works.

But this time it didn't work. The northern wind was too much for me, so with some reluctance my companions and I loaded up our fish and our boat and started for home. I remember wondering on the way home if I had overdone it. Had I been a bit overzealous in hauling the boat up the hill on its trailer? Because, quite obviously, the energy was still not there. But I never gave it another thought.

That night Calder got to wear Moby, the lunker amulet. This is a clay model of a fish suspended by fishing line, awarded to the person who catches the largest fish of the day. Calder quoted a favourite line from *A River Runs through It*: "The Lord has been good to us today, but he has been better to some than to others."

"I have an idea that the Lord just felt sorry for you, Calder."

I am the most fanatic devotee of brook trout I've ever known, so when a buddy of mine outdoes me with my chosen species, I don't like to take it sitting down. Calder was unfazed by my sarcasm. He stood omnipotent by the crackling stove before Paul and Julie Bidwell, wearing his amulet. I thought at the time that he had come a long way in his recovery from a heart attack exactly a year before. It seems to me, now, that the whole month of September had been echoing with mementos mori.

I woke up early to the sound of a very eager woodpecker and went out into the kitchen to make coffee and get the fire going in the stove. With the aroma of fresh coffee curling into the bedrooms of his cabin, Calder emerged. We decided not to hurry breakfast, to let Paul and Julie sleep in a bit. We had already promised to spoil them. No cooking, no excessive chores. Just lots of fishing and a high old time.

I left Calder sipping his coffee and bringing in the morning. I walked down the road, hoping, I suppose, to see another grouse. I didn't have my gun with me, but I had my trusty rabbit stick. I could hear the occasional drumming, and I thought (incorrectly, as it turned out) that there must have been a ruffed grouse very close at hand. I also had a bird book along with me, because I wanted to identify the woodpecker I had heard earlier. I rounded the bend in the road and beheld an immense woodpecker. It was he who had been doing the drumming, almost as though it were spring again and the rut was on.

He was a pileated woodpecker, a sort of chain saw with feathers. He was sending the chips flying in his search for ants in a big rotting tree. He would occasionally send a sharp *kuk* to his mate and then continue with his dismantling of the tree. Again, as the ancient mariner did to the water snakes, I blessed him unaware.

As I walked away, the woodpecker called to his mate: *whucker whucker whucker.*

Nature's great extrovert. I thought of Kramer from *Seinfeld.*

I was walking through a large sand pit surrounded by pines. I scooped up some dried mushrooms and looked down to examine them in my hand. Without the slightest warning, there was a puddle of blood in my hand. In a second or two, as I flung the mushrooms away, I knew that this was not just a nosebleed. I jammed a tissue into my right nostril and headed for home.

It was a walk of about six hundred yards. The tissue seemed to have no effect in staunching the flow, and as I walked I began to swallow a steady stream of blood. I dropped my rabbit stick on the front porch and walked into the cabin. Bob was sipping coffee and listening to the radio. Paul and Julie were still fast asleep in their bedroom.

I said to Bob, "I think we've got a problem."

Calder knocked on the Bidwells' door. Julie came out quickly in her pajamas, saw at once that I was having a bad bleed and got me to press down with a cool washcloth on the area where the blood seemed to be coming from. She put together an ice pack and began to apply pressure. Without so much as a yawn or a sigh, she was all business and completely in charge. The bleeding began to abate somewhat. I could tell this because I was swallowing less blood. Paul came out of the bedroom, still adjusting his clothes. Julie left to get dressed. When she returned, she asked about the nearest medical facilities and the nearest doctors, and by phoning around she quickly discovered that up around Little Bear, there were none.

The bleeding seemed to be getting under control, so without panic Julie continued phoning to find out where the nearest medical clinic was. There was one in Smeaton, but it wasn't open on Saturday. Smeaton was about an hour's drive south. Julie phoned the hospital in the town of Nipawin. This was about an hour's drive from Smeaton. Yes, they told her, they were open for business.

We had to do this phoning. We had heard so much about the shutdown of rural medical centres in Saskatchewan that we couldn't take the chance of driving to one that didn't have a doctor and a functioning emergency unit.

A bad bleed seems to have its own agenda, its own unique set of vascular pressures. My bleed suddenly went into overdrive. It seemed to burst out of the pressure dam we had created for it and rushed down my throat as fast as I could swallow. I summoned Julie, and she urged Paul to get us south as fast as we could go.

I didn't entirely get the point. I knew this was serious, but I didn't know the medical reasons why. When Julie and Paul both helped me up from my chair, out of the cabin and into the car, I protested that I could make it on my own. When Paul hit the highway running, I reminded him that we weren't in so much of a hurry that he had to speed.

He sped. My department head had become Jacques Villeneuve. Julie said nothing about this transformation, as if she concurred that speed was of the essence.

I tried to lighten up the atmosphere with jokes. I still didn't quite get it.

"If we pass a church," I told them, "I want you to stop."

"Why do you want us to stop?" said Julie.

"I want the priest to say a Paternostril."

I got an appreciative chuckle, but Paul did not slow down. It was a long hour.

What I wasn't quite getting was this: if I happened, through excessive blood loss, to faint, I could drown in my own blood. Julie knew this. She must have told this to Paul, because somewhere between the cabin and the highway Paul went from a concerned friend with the John Goodman smile firmly in place to a man with one thing on his mind, our rendezvous with the ambulance from Nipawin.

The blood began once more to flow faster down my throat. I

must have begun to grasp, at least intuitively, the gravity of my situation. I began to flash on the grouse I had killed two days earlier, the bright red blood bubbling from its beak. The blood that flowed from my own beak. For the first time, perhaps, in my entire life as a hunter, I began to regret having taken the life of a lovely wild creature. Somewhere north of Smeaton, I began to pray. *Get me out of this one*, I said, *and I swear, I will never again shoot another creature.*

I had once been a good hunter. By this I mean that as a young man, I had pursued game with real passion. I had brought home my share of meat for the pot. I had even taken up deer hunting, and although my ability to bring down game with a gun had suffered with the advance of middle age, I was still very keen to be in on the kill. That all ended abruptly.

At last, just north of Smeaton, we spotted the ambulance. I had swallowed more blood than I ever want to remember, and I had begun to lose feeling in my forearms and legs. I had no idea why I was losing feeling in these areas. I must have supposed it had something to do with shock. I had been in shock once before, and when it happened, most of my blood seemed to rush to the area of my heart in such a way that my extremities turned cold and clammy.

This time, on my way to the stretcher, I was genuinely wobbly on my legs. The ambulance crew lifted me straight into their vehicle and strapped me in with my head elevated. Julie was relieved to find out that the ambulance personnel had a suction machine at their disposal. At the time I was oblivious to the importance of this—that if I were to lose consciousness, the attendant inside with me was equipped to revive me and prevent me from drowning in swallowed blood. In fact, this is perhaps what Julie and the ambulance crew were discussing when I was inside. Before the vehicle took off for the Nipawin Hospital, the attendant gave me oxygen.

His name was Kevin. His main job, I see now, was to keep me from getting too worried, because if I panicked, my heart rate would increase and an excess of blood would be pumped through my veins and out the broken vessel. Kevin's conversation turned to fishing. If that was a ploy, it was a good one.

At this time, Kever was coming down from the north. She was glad to be finished with her professional responsibilities. More than anything, she wanted a cup of tea. When she arrived at Bob's cabin on Little Bear, Bob opened the door.

"Catch any fish?" she said.

Calder could not supress his grin, and before Kever had heard a thing, he brought her over to the fridge and showed her his three-pound brookie. Then Bob put on a fresh pot of tea and began, as casually as he could manage, to tell Kever about my mishap. He did so as unemphatically as he could while Kever sipped her tea.

"All the way to the Nipawin hospital?" Kever said.

"They just want to be sure," Calder said.

They waited in the cabin for the phone call from Paul and Julie at the Nipawin Hospital. It came at 11:00 A.M.

Before they left the settlement, Bob told Judith and her dad about my arrival in hospital, and they remained behind. The hope at this point was that part of the weekend could be salvaged, that most or all of us would soon be back up at Bob's cabin.

Bob and Kever headed south for Nipawin.

"Why aren't Paul and Julie coming back up to your cabin right now?" said Kever.

"Oh," said Calder, as casually as he could manage, "I guess Carp didn't want to be left alone."

"Oh," said Kever, who like me was just beginning to get the point.

"Do you want Dr. Martens or Dr. Chernesky?"

I searched the face of the nurse in the emergency unit. In spite of our advance call, there was still no doctor.

"I don't know," I said. "Which one has had this sort of thing to deal with?" I pointed to my nose. I couldn't believe they hadn't lined up a doctor ahead of time. The reason became clear in a moment.

"We can't choose for you. You have to choose which doctor."

I'm sure there must be some reason for this regulation, which effectively ties the hands of the head nurse, but I still haven't been able to find one. I thought for a moment: Martens, Chernesky. Chernesky, Martens. The head nurse had mentioned Martens's name first. Maybe it was fate that Martens would be my doctor.

"Martens."

Dr. Martens had been at this hospital for scarcely one week. It was his first day off, but apparently (being on call) he was already attending to an emergency case just a few feet from where I lay. He came in around noon and began to check me over. He was a big man, younger than me, and dressed casually in a weekend shirt and jeans. He looked like an athlete or a rancher or a construction worker—anything but a doctor. Immediately Martens ordered an IV to help compensate for the blood I had lost. Once he had located my leak, he began the painful process of plugging it. First he installed an inflatable device known as a Foley catheter. Once it was inflated inside my nasal passage, it began to cut off the various passages where blood could flow. This catheter was installed to dam up my blood, and to force it to slow down and clot. The catheter hung from my nostril, I imagine, like a sort of elephant's trunk. Martens also ordered some narrow tough surgical packing dipped in a saline adrenalin solution both to block and constrict the broken vessel. The more he tamped, the deeper the tape was lodged inside my nasal passages. I was given a shot of demerol and admitted to a ward. The idea was to move around as little as possible.

By the early afternoon I'd had a good chance to look around me. I was in quite a modern, cheerful facility. Perhaps this hospital was one of the ones threatened with closure earlier in the term of Romanow's NDP regime. A Grant Devine Hospital, in other words. I had voted for Romanow. I had agitated a great deal against former Premier Devine. Now I was here, as Paul Bidwell would say, by Devine intervention.

My situation was still very tense. Julie and Paul never left my side. A measure of the gravity of my situation was the fact that when Julie took my hand to reassure me, I would not let go. I clung to her as though she were a secret source of life.

When Kever arrived with Calder, Paul was there to brief her about my condition before she actually saw me. Nevertheless, she was unprepared to see me with what looked like a beached jelly-fish covering part of my face. For a terrible second, she thought that it was some sort of deformity, but it was just a collapsed plastic bag with ice cubes and a wash rag inside.

She and Calder and Paul and Julie remained in my room or just outside it, and much to my relief, the nurses allowed them to stay, even in the emergency unit. This facility had the friendly appeal of country hospitality.

I think, because I was in shock, my system was beginning to shut down and go into emergency mode. I was still losing feeling in my limbs. I couldn't move my bowels. I couldn't urinate. My bladder began to swell until, as they used to say in simpler times, my back teeth were floating. I can try to tell this with a certain measure of humour, but at the time there was nothing funny about the way I felt. In spite of my fears of such devices of torture, I called for a urinary catheter.

The nurses attending me were of the opinion that if I stood up, I would be able to ease my bladder. They were of course trying to spare me some pain. With an audience of several friends, I was hauled to my feet and given a bottle to pee into. Not only could I not pee, the jostling involved in getting me to my feet caused another bleed. Martens was summoned, but unfortunately he was attending to his case in the intensive care unit. The blood had found an opening in my plugged nostrils. First came a massive clot the size of a big leech worming down my throat; then came the blood under terrific pressure. I gulped and I gulped and then, for the second time that day, I prayed.

I know. There are no atheists in a sinking ship. But when you've resorted to all the usual avenues from medical cures to health insurance, and you're still in a state of distress, you turn to the last resort. The most entirely irrational one. I looked up at the people in the room and I was overcome by a sort of tenderness for them. Two nurses, Paul and Julie, Calder and Kever, and finally Dr. Martens. He increased the packing in my already crowded nostrils. This seemed to work for a minute or so, but then the blood began to seep through my tear ducts. My eyes glazed over with blood, and all the people in the room faded into rosy shadows.

After a while, a long while, it seemed, one eye cleared. In spite of my distress and the roseate hues cast over everything by the blood in my eye, I couldn't help but notice, again with something akin to tenderness, that everyone in the room wore the same concerned expression. All seven people, regardless of whether they knew me, wore the identical expression—and all seven were washed in the same rosy light. It was like a tableau out of antiquity. *Concern.*

Perhaps sometimes when you pray, you get people as a sort of answer. Their very presence and their need to bring comfort constitute a sort of spiritual medicine. I'm not trying to say that a miracle occurred here—only that this rosy tableau of concerned faces fed into my system in some way. My body seemed to get their message: *do what you can to get better.* From that point on, there was something going on inside me besides physical distress and fear. A sort of physical resolve to ride this one out. I began to resist the impulse to gulp my air; I began to breathe more easily.

This is not courage. This has nothing to do with mental toughness or anything else mental, nor has it anything to do with miracles. This resolve seemed to come both from my body and from the people gathered around my cot. Perhaps an audience bestows similar gifts on a stage actor. A loyal stand full of football fans can do the same for a losing team. (We from Saskatchewan know something of this.)

One of Dr. Martens's many virtues was that even at the worst of times he seemed unflappable. Everything he did seemed to be routine. Upon his arrival from South Africa he spent three years up north in Uranium City. My obdurate body functions were nothing new to him. He eased in the urinary catheter. As catheters always do, this one hurt like hell, but the results were as ecstatic as a wildcat strike. I gushed urine into my catheter tube, and the relief of the people gathered around me was audible.

"Well done, Carp."

"Good show."

"Bravo."

My friends were finally persuaded to disperse and return for the night to Bob's cabin, and early in the evening Kever was left alone with me. Thus began her vigil: September 16, 1995.

For some reason I was supposed to avoid liquids during that first night in the Nipawin hospital. My throat and esophagus were raw from the irritation of so much swallowed blood. I could only breathe through my mouth. These two things made my throat and mouth chronically dry. So I was given a container of ice cubes and allowed to suck on these all through the night. Anything warmer than ice cubes could have precipitated a worse bleed.

Kever found the room chilly. She crouched by my cot with a cotton thermal blanket over her head and body. I was supposed to lie perfectly still. I clung to the two middle fingers of her left hand. Whenever I had finished sucking another small ice cube, I would try to fall asleep. The dryness that racked my throat would awaken me. I would tug on the two fingers and Kever would lift my nose catheter and spoon in another ice cube.

For the first ten or twenty ice cubes, I whispered, "Hank you." For the rest of the night, I merely squeezed her fingers. This woman. This wife of mine. With the white thermal blanket over her head and body, she looked vaguely Iranian.

I will never forget this picture. It's my most recent proof for the existence of love. A small epiphany of sorts, like the moment when I flashed on the grouse bleeding from the beak, or the moment when I viewed the seven people at my bedside through rose-tinted eyeballs. I didn't see any reflections of Mary, Mother of Christ, for example, or Mary Magdalen. Instead I saw my wife looking as Muslim as the night is long.

Dr. Martens made rounds the next morning. In spite of all our efforts to keep my blood in its place, there had been more bleeding. I think I know why. It was probably a combination of strenuous exercise, some red wine the night before the bleed and the aspirin I had taken a couple of days earlier. In all likelihood the aspirin and the wine had acted to remove some of the stickiness from the platelets in my bloodstream and thereby prevented clotting. I was temporarily out of danger, but Martens decided that I should return to my ENT specialist in Saskatoon as soon as I could. Before we had time to inform the others up at Bob's cabin, I was loaded onto an ambulance for Saskatoon. Kever would have to try to follow behind in our car. I say "try" because she hadn't slept the entire night. By this time I was as worried about Kever as I was about my own condition.

When my ambulance passed the village of Weirdale, I lost sight of Kever. After about forty-five minutes on the road, Kever had had to pull off and catch a few winks at the picnic grounds in Weirdale. Perhaps she managed to doze a few minutes in the car. Soon she decided to drive on to Prince Albert. If she could grab a cup of tea, she might be able to stay awake long enough to drive herself to Saskatoon.

She only just made it to the McDonald's restaurant in Prince Albert. As she was walking towards the main door—this could only happen in Saskatchewan—she ran into Judith Wright and her dad. They too were on their way down to Saskatoon. She was saved.

When I arrived at St. Paul's Hospital, my own ENT doctor was not on call. Instead I was attended by Dr. Will, a partner of Peter Spafford's. He was well named, a take-charge sort of guy. First, as the nurses were gathering, he urged me to breathe slowly, to relax.

The procedure he was about to do was going to hurt a bit, and it was going to feel very uncomfortable. I could help, he told me, by not struggling and by not doing anything that would increase my heart rate. Don't panic, in other words.

I was wondering where Kever might be, if she were okay. It seemed to help, to get out of myself a bit, so I resolutely worried about Kever.

Dr. Will began by yanking out a goodly length of Dr. Martens's blood-soaked packing. As my bleeding resumed, he removed some massive clots and began to probe for my broken vessel.

"See?" he said to me. "Here it is."

In response, I spat out a huge clot into the Petri dish.

"Well done!" he said. And then. "Cocaine?"

I was about to shake my head. I assumed that he was inquiring as to whether I had a drug habit. But he was speaking to the nurse. Instead of the saline and adrenalin solution favoured by the physicians up at Nipawin, Dr. Will would use the cocaine for his packing. Cocaine, I learned, promotes vasoconstriction. In went the newly powdered packing, yards of it. Then a good shot of Demerol in the rump and what must have been a huge tablet of Valium, perhaps as big as a cookie.

Well, maybe I exaggerate. Maybe the rest of this day's activities will unfold before you in a hyperbolic fashion, because from this point on, I was as stoned as a New Age prophet. When Kever finally made it to Saskatoon, thanks to the good services of Judith Wright and her dad, Kever came immediately to my ward. She spoke with me a while and discovered that I was scarcely able to speak, owing to my well-stuffed, well-powdered nose. Referring to my eyes, she said later, "He looked so vulnerable. Like a deer caught in the headlights of a car."

Kever headed for home and sleep.

I stayed stoned and more or less awake as the light faded in my semiprivate. I was back in the safe embrace of St. Paul's Hospital once again, where old men drift around the wards like disembodied spirits.

Around this time a lovely young blonde woman showed up with a male friend.

"How *are* you, David?" she said, and tried to introduce me to her boyfriend. "Remember me?" she went on.

I hadn't the faintest idea who she was. I was expecting to see my doctor. I only wished this woman would go away. I began to struggle to sit up in bed. It seemed the polite thing to do.

"How are you feeling?" she said.

The second I achieved an upright position in the cot, a large blood clot began to gurgle down my throat. I fumbled for my emergency button to summon the nurse.

"Nod sho goo," I said, and mumbled something about expecting to see my doctor. My two visitors must have assumed that I needed *any* doctor. They both fled the room in search of a doctor and I never saw them again. The nurse came right in and gave me another shot of Demerol to slow down my heart beat and my blood flow. I lapsed back into my serenely stoned state. Mortality was drifting all through the hospital but I was safely steeped in my transcendent mode. It was the late sixties all over again.

I am sure that other people came to see me that evening and throughout the following days. A week later I left the hospital with twelve books, and I still can't remember who brought them all.

There's not much left to tell. My six nights in St. Paul's were more boring than nightmarish. My roommates came and went, each one after a day or two. They were invariably good company, and when they left for home I tried not to resent their good fortune.

I'm grateful to the nurses in Nipawin and at St. Paul's who kept returning to look in on me. What these overworked nurses would see was a pale middle-aged man with a blue plastic glass in his hand, sipping every five or ten minutes, all through the night. Frequently he was lost in a Demerol dream. He wore a moustache bandage just under his packed nostrils. Usually this bandage was itself flecked with blood and had to be changed frequently. The nurses always volunteered to give me a back rub, but I was afraid that the least little jostling would precipitate yet another bleed. I was probably right about this. I slept hardly at all.

On Saturday, September 23, Peter Spafford paid me one of several visits. By this time I was off the urinary catheter, off the iv. My bodily functions were slowly kicking into gear. Spafford had checked my hemoglobin, which was better than he had expected. Then he warned me that the next little procedure would hurt a bit. With his forceps he reached in and pulled out a few inches of packing. It came and it came, like line from a reel. A yard? Two yards? At last it lay coiled and blood soaked in my Petri dish. It looked like the world's longest tapeworm, smelly with putrefaction.

I waited for the warm descent of a big clot at the back of my throat and for the blood to well up and plunge down my throat again, but there was nothing. The air rushed sweet and icy up my nostrils. A pleasure almost worth dying for. Spafford viewed my nostrils with obvious pleasure. Dr. Will's emergency procedure had done nothing to disturb Spafford's delicate surgery.

"How am I doing?" I said in a voice so normal it sounded abnormal.

"You sure loused up my stats for the year," he said with a grin. "But it looks great up there. You're going home."

When you come back from a near-death experience, I am told, you might go through a sort of *Oh wow!* phase in which every friend, every falling leaf, every drop of rain, every dead skunk on the road is a sort of miracle of creation. My *Oh wow!* phase lasted one week. This was the week in which I began to discover the secret gifts of September. It began with my first night in bed with Kever. She had on new pajamas. The cat was purring between us. I could actually breathe through my nose.

When I came back from the hospital Kever pampered me. The first day after my return, a Sunday with no wind and a brilliant blue sky, she made lunch for us and we ate it on the patio. All through lunch we watched the birds in our garden. Wrens, finches, warblers, sparrows, chickadees, a pair of woodpeckers, a raucous blue jay. They all seemed to be gathering for a smorgasbord in our garden. Pecking away at the seeds and filling up for the long winter or for the voyage south. Dozens of them, hundreds. Our perpetually enthusiastic tabby was stalking them on this day.

"He's so bad," says Kever with obvious affection.

It's obvious our cat has made no deals with God about packing in his hunting career. For the first time in years I am just sitting with Kever and watching birds without the slightest intention of doing anything else. Lunch will take us all afternoon. Gus moves into the rhubarb patch and creeps under a huge rotting leaf.

"Look at him," I say. "Just waiting."

"He's bad," says Kever.

Legions of tiny birds continue to peck and then flutter away and flutter back again at a safe distance from our murderous young cat. The sun beats down strong on our exhausted garden. The sun will soon slip into the west and we'll wonder what became of it. We'll comment on how this fading light sneaks up on us. Count the *carpe diems*. They are everywhere.

These are the joys of September, to watch birds feed in our perilous garden on a warm day bracketed by chilly mornings and early sunsets. At times like this you know that September is almost as short as life itself.

The End of the Hunt

I HAVE A problem. As of last September, I have sworn off hunting. Kever and I are driving out to Togo on October 1 to visit with Doug and Barb Elsasser. How do I tell Doug, the greatest hunter I've ever known and my hunting buddy for years, that I have taken the pledge? All morning I've been rehearsing a conversation with him.

Ah, Doug, I begin.

Yeah?

We need to talk.

So? Talk.

That's as far as I've gotten.

The geese and ducks are driving me wild. Head off in any direction from Saskatoon, wherever you can find water. There they are, flocking and fattening up, getting ready to head south. More ducks than we've had in twenty-five years. I must learn anew how to *see* migratory fowl—in and for themselves as incomparably beautiful creatures. Not as so many succulent meals stuffed and trussed on a platter. Sounds nice on paper.

These are my thoughts as Kever drives us out to Doug and Barb's cabin. The weather is warm, the sky cloudless. The harvest is almost entirely off the fields, and it promises to be a good one. The year in Saskatchewan is coming to an end.

As we continue east of Kamsack, the Duck Mountains seem to rise up on the far horizon to greet us. They are hills, not mountains, but the blue ridge that forms them is so massive and sudden that they have the effect of mountains after such a wide expanse of prairie. Approaching the Duck Mountains from the west is a bit

like approaching the Cypress Hills from the north. The same sur-
prise awaits you.

We turn off Highway 5 and head south on the road to Coté
(pronounced Cody), Runnymede and Togo. This road runs
through a valley filled with ranches and farms that have preserved
a lot of wild brushland to the west and a huge forest reserve in the
park to the east. Real postcard scenery.

Doug and Barb's place is a rambling quarter that overlooks the
Lake of the Prairie. This lake is really a very long, dammed-up section of the Assiniboine River Valley. The view from the Elsassers'
cabin is expansive, to put it mildly. If you look southwest across
their ravine you can see the tip of one of their meandering fields.
Some days you can spot grazing elk. If you look south and east
from their kitchen you see, instead, the Assiniboine Valley. To the
north is a mixture of forest and community pasture. Straight
northeast is Duck Mountain Park. This means bear and moose
and lots of other wildlife, and an abundance of fish. Bass, muskies,
pickerel, pike and perch, and five species of trout.

Um, Doug, we need to have a talk.

About hunting? he will say.

Well, I suppose so, but it's not what you think.

Elsasser will give me a strange look.

Something has happened, I will say.

And then I will say . . .

Start over.

Doug, we need to have a talk.

He looks up from his cup of coffee.

Talk? About what?

The oldest October ritual in Saskatchewan that I know of is the
goose hunt. In Alberta, where the mallards are more plentiful, it
would probably be a duck hunt. But here in drought-prone
Saskatchewan there isn't always a plentiful supply of ducks; with
each decade, however, there seem to be more and more geese.
Lesser and greater Canadas, snow geese and specklebellies. The

majority of these birds nest up north where farmers can't drain their marshes for a bigger field of grain, and the geese gather in early September, the grown goslings and their parents, forming huge extended-family groups for the big migration south.

The most northerly nesters take their time. The forage is pretty good from well north of the Arctic Circle to the grainfields of southern Saskatchewan. We don't begin to see the huge flocks until towards the end of September. Conservationists who fight for the survival of endangered species have no worry about the wary geese. Since the early fifties their numbers in Saskatchewan have actually increased. Our prairie chicken is extinct, their habitat poisoned and ploughed away. Locals have since taken to calling the sharptail grouse a prairie chicken, but even this magnificent look-alike is on the wane.

Not so the wild geese. They honk their way north in March to bring in spring, and they honk their way back south in October to draw down the blinds of winter. For those two periods, their shrill voices are as familiar to our ears as the song of nightingales to the English or the mocking birds to the people of the Deep South. It makes sense. A region's birds come to stand in some mysterious way for that home place. Their calls seem to give voice to the very spirit of the place. And just as a nightingale might, in some way, come to embody the yearning spirit of rural English romanticism, so the cries of the wild geese give voice to an entire way of life up north.

They enter your territory, not gently like a songbird, but like a force of nature, a storm or a weather front. This high fierce barking is the voice of harsh necessity, a response to the violent contrasts of the seasons that run our lives. The sound emerges from a great feathered body with nearly a pound of goose fat to keep the bird insulated from the blizzards; it flows up the length of a long powerful neck with vocal cords as resonant as the inner workings of a Swiss horn. Out the beak it goes, hoarse, falsetto, urgent. Valkyries. An attack from the very gods.

My father raised my brother and me to hunt with him, just as his father raised him and his brothers, just as my mother's father raised his son to hunt. Every October in southern Saskatchewan. Both of these grandfathers came out from Ontario as young men at the turn of the century, and in both cases, when they learned of the great abundance of geese on the prairie, they took to the hunt as though it called to them from a long time ago when life (yes, even for the genteel Anglos) was tribal, and hunting was not a sport but a great need.

Think of it. We've been out of the woods for a thousand years or so, living in relatively stable communities enclosed by political boundaries. But we lived in the woods for two or three million years. An entirely tribal, pagan world is what we came from, and in hunting we can still communicate with that world, if only in rituals and faint re-enactments. I hasten to say, this communication doesn't happen to every hunter, but it happens to me and it happens to Doug Elsasser.

Never before in history has the annual hunt been so much under attack. Chemical companies are flourishing. International arms trade has never been hotter. Almost any industry involved in depleting the ozone layer (cars, air traffic, fossil fuels) seems to be thriving. But Canadians are massing against hunters as though they know something about evil that I simply can not grasp.

We hear a great deal about hunters who are incapable of responding to the wilderness as a powerul numinous presence. They drive all-terrain vehicles or hunt from power toboggans—anything to avoid walking and listening and *paying attention*. They bring ghetto blasters to their campsites and listen to sports news, deejays and their favourite ads. Regardless of the season these hunters will shoot pregnant cow moose or nesting ducks. They will shoot from pickups and abandon their quarry to rot. Or they leave wounded birds and animals to die a slow death in the bush. They kill a bear only for its gall bladder or a huge breeding elk just for his antlers. They scatter their garbage on the roads and campgrounds. In spite of years of practice, they handle their booze very badly.

These jerks are real enough. But they get all the publicity because they attract all the attention. Perhaps we've all met a few of them. Perhaps they are your next door neighbours. But rest assured, there are better hunters than these among us.

You almost never hear about the many women who join in the hunt year after year. This includes my university office mate, Maria Campbell. She and her daughters have hunted moose and deer through all the lean years of life in the north. Her ancestors are among the great hunters of this part of the world, so no one in Maria's family is aghast at a woman's love of the hunt.

You almost never hear about the depth of appreciation in the hearts of ordinary urbanites for the hunt. I have hunted with friends who go out one or two weekends a year, who call themselves sportsmen, who wear plaid shirts from designer catalogues, who live in the heart of an urban sprawl; and among them all, something awakens out there in the goose pit or the woods that is so entirely primitive that on a good morning it brings up those vestigial hairs on the back of the neck.

Time and again I am asked the following question: What is the appeal of hunting to these city slickers?

Let me begin with the obvious. City life everywhere tends to create a need for its opposite. Too much noise creates a need for quiet. When the brain has to process too much information (video games, stock quotes, computer data, TV shows), it yearns simply to *think*. Too much fast food or processed meat creates a need for something healthy. An almost entirely domestic world creates a yearning for the wild earth. The body wants to live again.

This will sound preposterously romantic, but there was a time when we used our noses and ears for day-to-day survival. Perhaps someone inside us, wiser than we have become in the city, wants to tear off that Walkman and listen to a stream gurgle or a chickadee call. Someone inside us wants to rediscover excuses to pay attention.

On a hunting trip you tend to pay attention. You notice which way the wind is coming from. When you stalk animals, you need to approach them with the wind in your face. You come to learn that certain birds take off and land into the wind. You examine footprints carefully. You study fallen trees, large rocks and other landmarks and remember them or you tend to get lost. You smell things—at first, because you can't help it. But then you come to rely on your sense of smell to perform dozens of little tasks. You walk quietly because you have to, and when you do this, you begin to hear the tiniest sounds and you learn to identify them. A whole world begins to return to you, a world that becomes more and more sacred the more it is ravaged by mindless human expansion.

Another question I get asked is this: To attain this dramatic state of awareness do you have to go out and kill something?

I always say, of course not. Many hunters, myself included, eventually foresake the gun and find other excuses for getting back into the bush. These older hunters are glad to leave the killing to the young. It is a specific feeling they are hunting for. Hunters are addicted to it: that surge of well-being that comes over a man or woman when the senses are on full alert, the body in motion, the mind focussed. As your senses return to you, walking in the cold fall air, something hits you like a drug, a second wind of epic proportions, the ultimate jogger's high. Your body becomes infused with a strange and powerful flow of energy, many times more powerful than you thought you might possess. The need to stay warm promotes the need to keep moving, and ordinarily walking long distances would make you tired, but because all your senses are focussed on the pursuit of your prey (to hunt it or simply to see it), your body becomes strangely energized.

I'm now in my fifties, and I find that a four-mile walk in the city is taxing. But every time I go hunting I discover that day after day, I can cover twenty miles or more and return from the experience fit as can be. In my case, under the right circumstances, this surge of energy comes on the very first day out.

Another frequent question: How could you bear to pull the trigger on those beautiful creatures when you claim to love the wilderness? How are you any different from anyone else who destroys our environment?

This question is the most frequent and bespeaks the most innocence. The question presupposes that there are two kinds of people: those who destroy the environment and those who leave it alone. The people who ask this question will often place hunters on one side of the moral fence (with developers, weapons manufacturers, producers of farm chemicals and other such villains) and themselves on the other side (with vegetarians, ecologists and urban protesters of all kinds).

Perhaps someone told them that one is either part of the problem or part of the solution. Remember that argument?

Many of these same people will wear leather goods. They will shop for hunks of dead meat at a mall (which they will refer to by the comfortable name of "groceries"). They will never learn or want to learn what it is like for steers or pigs to line up at the abbattoir watching the animal in front of them being electrocuted. Fear of violent death elicits a peculiar smell, and pigs are especially sensitive to that smell in the abbattoir. They frequently die in a state of terror.

Hunters live with a paradox that very few nonhunters understand: they prowl through wilderness in order to kill the creatures that they love. This paradox helps to explain why hunters are such strong conservationists. If you recycle religiously, contribute time or money to environmental causes and are a vegetarian, environmentally speaking, you have the moral high ground and my respect. But bear in mind that a true hunter is like any other passionate lover of the wilderness. Call him (or her) your enemy if you will, but most hunters would never dream of destroying natural habitat.

When you fish and hunt with any regularity, you also become involved in a host of other equally healthy activities. You learn how to marinate grouse meat, how to prepare butterflied trout, how to dress and roast a mallard. But before you can do any of these wonderful things, you need to learn how to gut or pluck or field dress or clean your quarry. You learn what kind of animals and birds provide good meat. You learn which meat is better pickled, which is better smoked. You gain an intimacy with the food that may well feed you all winter long. Never again will you take good food for granted as you have in the past. Never again will you make the mistake of assuming that food comes painlessly in packages. In every North American city I've ever seen, there are always commercial forces at work that serve to distance you from the food you eat. Food becomes exotic. Food becomes someone else's business. Food becomes anything but bloody. If there's any virtue in this process of obscuring our vision of the things we eat, I have yet to discover it.

Lately, over the past six or seven years, I've been missing a lot of shots. My mind is engaged with the hunt, but my body finds itself moving in a contrary fashion. The goose flies *this* way, and so the body should move in such a way as to line up the bird and fire. But my body wants to go *that* way. It wants to do something else. During recent trips I catch myself waiting, waiting, when I should be shooting. The mind knows this, but the body seems to know something else.

Carp, shoot! comes the cry of my exasperated friends.

What is my body doing, exactly?

For one thing, it's watching the bird. How close will it come this time? How old is this one? Is it a lesser Canada or a specklebelly? When will it discover me under this blind? Let's wait and see.

I don't want to shoot things anymore; it's come to that.

Some years ago, when the geese were almost as prolific as they are now, Doug Elsasser, Jack Gilhooly and I went on a goose hunt to Sceptre. This village is a four-hour drive southwest of Saskatoon. When we got there, we had to confirm the location and the flight patterns of a good-sized flock we had found.

I can remember this hunt as though it happened last fall. We are parked in a straggle of trees under the shadow of the Great Sand Hills. About three thousand geese are feeding in the stubble of a recently harvested field of barley. We take turns spying on them through a pair of field glasses. Back and forth the geese go in groups of up to a hundred birds: from our field to a big slough nearby, and from the slough back to the field. A fat noisy gaggle if ever I've seen one. We secure permission to dig pits on the farmer's land. By the time it grows dark, at least a thousand of them are still feeding there. Some snow geese and lesser Canadas, but mostly specklebellies.

At last we get out of the car and trudge across the field, spades in hand. When we reach a dip about two hundred yards from the edge of the remaining flock, they all take off in a histrionic explosion of goose outrage.

"They'll be back," says Doug.

It's too dark to see exactly where the birds have been concentrating. By this I mean the very centre of feeding activity. So Doug hauls a flashlight out of his knapsack and begins to pace along the stubble in search of the greatest concentrations of gooseshit. At Elsasser's bidding, we begin to dig our three holes, side by side. We have to guess that the wind will again come from the northwest, so we dig the holes in such a way that we will all be side by side in a row facing the geese as they come in, rather than one behind the other. The geese will likely return from their water for a morning feed by circling our pits and landing into the wind. In other words, they will come from the southeast.

The holes take a long time to dig. There is little talk and much puffing. Gilhooly is getting antsy.

"Remember," he says, "bar closes in two hours."

Doug looks over at Gilhooly like a plumber examining a particularly vexing problem with a sewer drain. Doug likes it if you take an interest.

Gilhooly yawns, Doug frowns, and the three of us return to the silent business of digging holes.

After a long sweaty time of it, the holes are finished and Doug dispatches Gilhooly and me to round up a big pile of straw. We scatter the straw all around our three holes and toss the rest inside. Then we cover our holes with boards.

The night is a bit too warm for October. We would prefer to have a stormy wind and low overcast skies. In fact, the forecast is for rain and cooler weather. But tonight the breeze remains resolutely mild and the stars come out one by one. Out on the big slough nearby, the geese gab and cackle by the thousands. They are having a high old time.

Someone's alarm is ringing, and I haven't the faintest idea whose it is or why some demented sonofabitch would set off an alarm clock in the middle of the jeezly night. It isn't *my* alarm clock. I've got enough on my mind without this damned machine. I've been arguing with this pigbrained slug of an editor about my title. It's a good title. He insists that I change it to the one his girlfriend likes. My title is pure poetry: *The Floating Kisses of Eden.* The one his girlfriend likes is such a cornball title no publisher in his right mind would accept it: *Going Stacey's Way.*

Going Stacey's Way? You've gotta be kidding! For one thing, there's no one named Stacey in the entire book. Look! Check it out! Not one trace of a Stacey!

"Well, maybe if you get out of bed, Carp, you'll find her in the coffee shop."

Doug Elsasser is standing over me. He is holding a big duffle bag directly over me. He is about to drop the bag on top of my head. He drops it on top of my head.

"Come, Sah'b, we are not wanting to be late for the maharishi. I have saddled your elephant."

This voice belongs to Gilhooly. This morning he is a mahout.

It turns out that we are up too early for the coffee shop to be open, but Elsasser has already covered this contingency. There's a pot of coffee brewing in our little room. And a plate full of doughnuts. He is dressed, arranging his shells on the bed. He takes one kind and slips them into his cartridge belt and then dumps the rest into his jacket pocket. He turns to me.

"Eat."

At such times, when the urgency of the hunt is on him, Elsasser becomes something beyond taciturn. He becomes a combination of Sergeant Rock and Big Bear. Nods, hand signals, one-syllable words. *Hurry. Geese fly at dawn.*

Gilhooly is his opposite. This morning he sings a selection of Johnny Cash in his newly fashioned mahout's accent. "I am falling in to a bahning ring of fire, I am going down down down as the flames are going higher."

"Can it, Gilhooly."

"And it is bahning bahning bahning, dis ring of fire—"

"Enough!"

The doughnuts and the coffee go down fast and delicious, as though they were destined to be the last comfort from civilization. I have a feeling it's going to be cold. The wind is up. It vibrates the basement shutters. On go the long johns and wool socks, on go the wool shirt and the sweater, on go the canvas pants and canvas hunting jacket.

"Could be wet, Carp."

Off comes the canvas hunting jacket. On goes the rain gear, top and bottom. Back on goes the jacket. On goes the canvas cap. On go the boots. We trudge like football players down the hall and out into the street. The street is covered with snow.

"Snow!"

"Snow?"

"My gracious heavens, not since the Khyber Pass have I beheld such—"

"Gilhooly, enough awready!"

It is only a five-mile drive to our pits, but will the water be open? In other words, will our geese still be there when we arrive? If so, will they feel disposed to land among our decoys for a last feed before heading to Texas?

We park in the trees, and the whole scene is almost unrecognizable. The branches of the trees and bushes are feathered with snow, the ground is covered with several inches of powder. The visibility is not good, but better than I had expected, because everything seems to glow in the dark. We load up with decoys, shells, food and thermoses of tea, and move out in single file towards our pits. Fortunately, Doug has marked them by shoving sticks into the ground by each hole. The wind sweeps across the field like Doom itself.

When the wind falls, I catch the rising babble of goose talk. Once in a while there is the dissident quack of a lone duck.

"Let's move it!" says Elsasser in an urgent whisper.

We arrive at the pits with the aid of Doug's flashlight. I choose the left pit and Gilhooly takes the right one. Elsasser shakes out the decoys. He will take the middle pit and call the whole hunt. We place most of our decoys in front of our holes, some heads into the wind, some pointing elsewhere. Elsasser discovers that we have laid some of them in too regular a pattern, so he disperses a dozen or so. We are down into our pits before we know it. Over our heads goes a bundle of straw about as wide as a sombrero. All I can see is the pure white field before us and the fringe of trees that separates us from the big slough full of birds.

And then the sound of Doug's goose call. A bassoon warming up? A clarinet blown by your mischievous little brother? Anyway, a very ragged sound.

"The slough is twelve o'clock," whispers Elsasser, after a few honks. "The truck is six o'clock."

"Ah don lak it owt thar, boys. It's too quiet."

Gilhooly has become Slim Pickins as an old Marine.

Something seems to rise above the trees to the right.

"One o'clock," I whisper.

"Get down," says Elsasser.

I crouch down into my pit so that my shotgun barrel is poking up into the straw that covers the entrance. Then comes the noise of approaching birds, a high frantic barking.

"Carp, three goosks coming in from behind. You'll have to turn around."

I come up slowly from my crouch, ease off the straw and spot them. Three geese, flying low across the decoys. They drop down from tree height, and because of the semi-dark and the renewed snowfall, they can scarcely make out what I am. My head pokes out of a straw-covered hole. I could be just another goose having breakfast in the snow. They drop even lower and set their wings. This manoeuvre looks a bit like an airplane coming down to a landing strip in a high wind. A wing dips, the bird tilts sideways, it rights itself. All three geese do this in unison: dipping, tilting, flapping back to the horizontal. You can get mesmerized by the acrobatics of it. Then the wings set in a downward curve. *This* is the moment when those vestigial hairs stand up on the back of my neck.

"Now," says Elsasser.

The time is 8:15 A.M. The snow has stopped falling and the sun is up, though still not visible. We have shot our limit of fifteen birds, plus a couple of mallard drakes. Weighted down with them, we move off the field. A very good morning.

"I've got this friend who always winters in Mexico," says Elsasser. "A biologist from Mississippi. He keeps asking me why I don't come down there and escape the cold. I can talk till I'm blue in the face, and he just doesn't understand."

Elsasser is beaming. He always looks this way after a successful hunt. The smile emerges because he can no longer hide his satisfaction.

After breakfast at the café we head back out to the Sandhills. The sun is shining and the snow melting. The tops of the sand dunes are already free of snow and the air is cool and sweet with the smell of sage and stubble. Doug parks his truck and begins to set up the process of plucking, which will take us a good two or three hours. I'm not looking forward to this.

First, Elsasser goes into his truck and puts on a big pot of water and paraffin to boil on a camp stove. This pot is for the birds. You dip them into the paraffin, let it dry on the feathers and then pull off the wax, feathers and all. But even after the paraffin has done its work, there are still many feathers to pull. The idea is to make it all enjoyable.

The next step is to find a nice dry spot up on the Sandhills. The view must be exactly right. Doug and Gilhooly choose a high dune with a south-facing view of row upon row of Sandhills. We can see so far south that we imagine we can make out the northeastern edge of Montana.

We each grab a bag of geese and climb up to the top of the dune. Elsasser lines us up so that we are side by side, as we were in the pits. Between himself and his two plucking buddies, Elsasser places two opened, chilled bottles of *haut sauterne*. He pushes each bottle into the sand and then packs snow around it. Then he lays down cushions for us to sit on.

"Got your harp?" he says to Gilhooly.

"Yep."

And so the morning plucking begins. We tear off the feathers, dip and scrape, then gut the birds. As we work, we swig from the nearest bottle. Since Doug is in the middle, he has the privilege of drinking from either bottle. Wine in the morning. How did I become such an epicurean?

After we've plucked and cleaned a half-dozen birds or more, Gilhooly pulls out his harp and begins to play. This is a blues harp, of course, a mouth organ, for those of you who haven't yet become blues aficionados. Gilhooly begins with a slow stately hymn, "Just a Closer Walk with Thee." He sucks his notes out of the little holes and bends them, sends them mournfully in the direction of New Orleans.

My bottle of wine has acquired a downy neck. This is only a bit disgusting. The wine gets better and better as the day wears on. The breeze is at our backs. It lifts the goose down from our laps and drifts feather after feather towards Montana.

"America," Elsasser calls, Paul Revere to the hunters. "The goosks are coming. The goosks are coming."

"Doug, we need to have a talk."

We are sitting out on Doug and Barb's veranda. Kever and Barb are stretched out on their deck chairs, eyes closed to the warm sun. Already since breakfast we've heard some elk bugling just below the rim of the valley. A perfect morning.

"Is this guy-to-guy talk?" Doug says in a lazy voice.

"Fraid so."

"Well, if you two want to have a guy-to-guy talk," says Barb, "we are not movin."

She says this through closed eyes, stroking their dog, Brewer. Brewer opens one sleepy eye, yawns and closes his eye again.

"Let's go, Carp," says Doug. "I have to put out some leech traps. You can come along for the ride."

"And don't let him lift anything," says Kever.

She is protective of my health. Doctor's orders. Lie still and no vigorous movement. As my blood supply builds up, I go everywhere slowly, like a very old man.

Doug and I climb into Old Blue, a truck he's had since he was in his late teens. His leech-gathering equipment has been loaded into the back. He sells these leeches to bait and tackle stores which in turn sell most of them to anglers in pickerel tournaments. It's a good sideline for Elsasser, because these days the stores pay well.

We head on down through the gate and out across the road to a valley filled with small marshes. Perfect for leech gathering. Doug slows down at the wheel and begins to survey the nearest little slough.

"Okay, Carp. What's on your mind?"

"Our annual hunt."

"Good. I had a few ideas. Amazing hatch this year. Imagine that. Thousands of goosks right around here."

"Yeah."

I take a big breath and turn to face Elsasser. He continues to stare out at the slough where he will lay down his first line of leech traps.

"Something happened up north," I begin.

"So I heard."

"Yeah, but I mean in addition to the bleeding and stuff."

Elsasser turns to face me. He wears a skeptical look, almost hostile, as though I'm about to announce that I'm going to run for the leadership of the Conservative Party of Canada.

"Have you ever been scared?" I ask him.

Elsasser is close to scoffing. "Well, I suppose I've been in situations where I couldn't let on how I was feeling."

"I'll take that as a yes?"

"Get to the point."

"One more question, Elsasser."

He sighs.

"When you look out at all this, the big hills, the Assiniboine Valley, all the deer, all these marshes and meadows, do you ever get to thinking what might have created it all?"

The skeptical lines of his face shift from a 'don't tell me you're runnin for the Conservatives' look to a 'don't tell me you've been born again' look.

He says, grudgingly, "Yeah?"

"What do you call it?"

"Well, Carp, I guess I'd call it the Creator."

"Great!"

Elsasser swears under his breath.

"When I was coming down in the car, things got sort of weird. The bleeding got kind of bad."

"So?"

"Well, I got quite worried at one point, because I was gulping blood. I mean, too much blood."

"Yeah?"

"So. I said, like, a prayer. To the Creator."

"Yeah?"

"And I said that if He could get me out of this one alive, I'd promise never again to—"

"Oh, fuck."

"—shoot another creature."

Elsasser scowls at the gas pedal. He says, "Can I interrupt this to talk a little sense into you?"

"Go ahead."

"How did you word it? What word did you use?"

"You mean in my—"

"Yeah. Did you say fishing too?"

"Elsasser, I was worried. I wasn't crazy."

"So it's just hunting?"

"Shooting. I said I'd never shoot anything again."

"Well, does that include a bow and arrow? A rabbit stick?"

"Yeah. I think so."

"But it doesn't include fishing?"

"You don't shoot fish."

Without a word, Elsasser climbs out of the truck and begins to lay his leech traps. I watch him as he goes. When he returns to the truck, he starts it up and doesn't speak for several minutes, not until we reach the top of the next grade.

"Well, Carp, I guess when you make a promise like that, you've got to keep it."

"Yeah."

"I mean, not that you had to worry all that much."

"What do you mean?"

"Well, the last few times out you couldn't hit the broad side of a barn door. I mean, hell, what is it exactly you've given up on?"

"There's no need to be sarcastic."

That day in October was one of the loveliest times I've ever spent, not hunting, in my entire life. Kever loved it in the same sweetly idle way. Doug and Barb planned a picnic supper for when the heat of the day had passed. They loaded up the car with various necessaries, including a roasted goosk carefully packed away in the back trunk. Doug had shot it only a week earlier. As we drove into the heart of the Duck Mountains, the aroma of goose in the roaster moved all through the car and drove us mad with hunger.

We arrived at the shores of a small deep lake surrounded by big hills and pine forest. It had heavy marshes all around the side and a small dock for canoes. We brought out the supper and the folding chairs just as the sun was beginning to set. Barb poured the wine, and with our eyes on the water, we all tucked into our Thanksgiving meal. Doug had stuffed the bird with a hot curry that made me think, oddly, of Gilhooly.

I spotted a rise near the dock, and then another rise.

The supper was almost too perfect to spoil with conversation, but I said, "I swear I saw a trout rise."

"Where?"

Just as I started to point, another trout rose, this time only several yards from shore, a good one this time.

"What's in this lake?" I said.

"Thought you'd never ask," said Doug, grinning. "Some rainbows and brookies."

"You're kidding."

We ate our curried goose and looked on in astonishment as the trout continued to dimple the surface. An October rise. It was almost a contradiction in terms. It felt like it might be the last warm day of the year and the very last rise as well.

"Too bad we didn't bring our fishing gear," I said.

There was a knowing silence, conspiratorial.

"Actually," said Kever.

"You're kidding."

Doug opened up the trunk again and took out an armload of fishing tackle. There was still time, maybe forty-five minutes before complete darkness.

"If you promise not to exert yourself," said Kever.

"I promise."

It had been almost three weeks since I had come home from

hospital, and I hadn't had enough energy even to walk around the block. But now, with the day and the warm weather fading so beautifully, I felt a tiny surge of youth.

In another existence, perhaps I would have said no to fishing and just sat in my chair and savoured the sunset and the goose curry belches and had an aesthetically satisfying moment and maybe thought briefly but deeply about mortality and life's seasonal rhythms. But of course, having learned early on that the path to hell was paved with unfished lakes, I foresook my lawn chair.

I joined Kever and Barb and Doug, casting from the shore of the tiny lake. In twenty minutes we had four trout. The largest was a sixteen-inch male brookie, dazzling in dark olive and bright orange.

The day, the meal, the fishing, the people, even my confessional conversation with Elsasser and his leech traps—it had all felt like a continuous offering of thanksgiving. I had even extracted a promise from Elsasser that I would be welcome on his future hunts as a bird dog, game cleaner, cook and plucker. I've been called worse.

Conclude with the obvious. The best thing about October is Thanksgiving. For many, it's the end of the harvest. It's the end of all that wonderful fall weather, the end of a whole year in Saskatchewan. The pause before winter that says thank-you to life for life.

Epilogue:
The Bozone Layer

I've been pondering a quotation from Ken Kramer and his wife, Sue (now deceased), both of whom spent years of hard work and fruitful effort with the Globe Theatre in Regina.

> *Saskatchewan is not a wonderful place in which to live. The winters are too cold and long, the summers are too hot and short. It is cheaper to live here than in most places in Canada, but one's salary is also lower than in those places. So why do we stay? We stay because there is a spirit in Saskatchewan which grows wheat in a desert, which grows trees where no trees ever grew, and which produces a quality of person that is unique, daring and altogether a puzzle to the rest of the country.*

For weeks now, I've been troubled by this ambivalent declaration of loyalty to life in Saskatchewan. For one thing, it gives credit for some dubious environmental practices. I wouldn't want to go down in history for growing wheat in a desert. This practice makes for two things: lousy yields and beautiful desert laid waste. And I don't see much difference between the quality of people in Saskatchewan and those in any other part of the world. The only reason I can think of that Saskatchewan people might be "a puzzle to the rest of the country" is that no one comes here to see them. If you come to think of Saskatchewan in the above terms, given the right financial incentives, you're just as likely to end up leaving it.

Here's a more reliable testimony to the virtues of Saskatche-wan. And it comes to us from some people who have chosen to stay here. When Paul and Julie Bidwell arrived in Saskatoon in 1966, Julie said to Paul, "I can manage two years out here, but then I want us go back to Ontario." A few years later, she said to Paul, "Okay, I'll live here, but I'm not going to grow old here." Some time in the 1970s Julie said to Paul, "All right, I can imagine grow-ing old here, but not dying here. I want to end my days in Ontario." In the 1980s she confessed to Paul that, well, yes, maybe she could imagine dying here, but she would want her remains to return to Ontario. Not long ago, Julie confided to Paul that she *could* imagine being buried out here, perhaps somewhere near the South Saskatchewan River.

I've got an idea. Hop in the car and drive with me to the edge of the city of Saskatoon. Any clear night will do. We'll head off into the Minichinas Hills, look up at the night sky, check out the galax-ies and the northern lights. Then we'll turn around and drive back down from the hills, and behold: Saskatoon, glowing at our feet like a vast constellation.

The thing that might strike you as unique is that *there is an edge* to my city. If you are from New York or Toronto or Montreal, you might have difficulty pointing to the edge of your city. Or even Vancouver. Its southern edge is maybe New Westminster, or maybe Ladner, Richmond or Delta. The eastern edge of Rich-mond and Delta is maybe Newton or Surrey. The eastern edge of Surrey is maybe Cloverdale or Langley. The eastern edge of Lang-ley is either Murrayville or Aldergrove. The eastern edge of Alder-grove is, surely, Abbotsford. After Abbotsford, you can probably tell where it stops and Chilliwack begins, but not from the Trans-Canada Highway. All I know is that for sure, ninety miles from Vancouver, in Hope, I have left Vancouver and its eastern exten-sions. If you are like me, and not fond of heavy traffic and urban sprawl, you'll see this Voyage to Hope almost entirely in spiritual terms.

I don't deny that Vancouver is a continual delight, especially for the pleasure-seeking urbanite who wants to live at a humane, much less than frantic pace. (I've never managed to have a non-pleasurable time in Vancouver.) I don't deny that Vancouver, as they say, has it all. But sometimes all can be way too much.

Trop de monde, as they say.

Given twenty years to live there, I could have written this book about Schenectady or Hamilton or Chilliwack. Or Red Deer, Sept-Iles, Brandon, Guelph, Rimouski or Fort Wayne, Indiana. By their seasons shall ye know them. By how their people react when the first frost arrives. Like all places, these ones become sacred, become beautiful, become *home* to those who will just get to know them; to those who become custodians over the land given in trust to them. But people all over the world can be such jerks.

Over the last few days I've been looking at an old Gary Larson cartoon. Several years ago I stuck it up on my wall. I used to think it was funny, but now I contemplate it as though it were hanging in a gallery of contemporary art. It's beautifully drawn. A part of the globe is just visible at the bottom of the picture. Curving above this segment of our globe is a layer of inner atmosphere, and above the inner atmosphere is a dense layer of people. They are so small that it takes a magnifying glass to see that this floating wall of people encircling the globe is made up entirely of clowns. Above the layer of clowns is the outer atmosphere, and above that is the moon. Larson's caption reads as follows: "The bozone layer: shielding the rest of the solar system from the Earth's harmful effects."

Why not? We have become such a species of bozos, we seem to infect every natural thing we touch, including our own atmosphere. The news of war, disease and famine declares that human life is cheap. More accurately, the *perception* is that human life is cheap. The headlines, the TV news and especially violent movies have inadvertently become a breeding ground for the new misanthropy.

For a long time I've struggled with my own lapses into this misanthropy. It begins with the following sequence of problems. Any progressive step forward these days for a group of people or a nation must also mean that yet another forest or another river or another tract of wilderness or another source of ozone must be destroyed. I was astounded to learn that Simon Reisman, our chief free-trade negotiator for the GATT talks with the United States, was an adviser to the Great Recycling and Northern Development scheme to dam a great many rivers that flow into James Bay and divert them all to the United States. His rationale for such a disruption of the northern communities and the northern environment was apparently that unharnessed waters are wasted. Wasted! When you keep company with bozos like this, you come to believe that all economic progress or worldly gain must of necessity include an earthly loss. Humankind in the mass becomes the great polluting blunder of creation. A huge contagion. Kudzu.

After my first day and night in the Nipawin hospital my misanthropic leanings began to suffer a serious setback. It took more than a dozen people just to begin the process of saving my life, and at least half of these people did not even know me. Like as not, they didn't even share my moral and political convictions. I was in a Grant Devine hospital, for God's sake!

So, I have some serious thinking to do. My misanthropy is clearly useless in the presence of such overwhelming evidence of a species so determined to *bring comfort* to a suffering person. During that awful time, this impulse to bring comfort was as palpable as the blood that ran down my throat.

I'm a member of the race that invented nuclear power but hasn't got a clue about what to do with the expended fuel. A race that gave birth to space travel but has not a clue as to how to clean up its garbage in space, its garbage at home. But the same race of humans is also possessed of the wisdom to love a place—even a forbidding place, as mine has been called.

It's January again. I'm trying to get going on a new quinzhee. But right now it's 31 below, and how can I justify inveigling my friends out of their comfortable nests to come over here and heave piles of snow into our back garden? For seventeen days, the temperature has hovered between 28 and 42 below. This is the second-worst prolonged cold snap in the history of the province. Tomorrow—if we're lucky and the weather is very cold—we will tie the all-time record for miserable winter weather. There are pessimists in our midst who say the weather will turn mild, that we haven't got a chance, but I remain hopeful. Now *that* is a true Saskatchewan affirmation.